# Reason
# &Rigor

*For our students, whose questions have inspired this book.*

# Reason &Rigor

## How Conceptual Frameworks Guide Research

Sharon M. Ravitch
Matthew Riggan
*University of Pennsylvania*

Los Angeles | London | New Delhi
Singapore | Washington DC

Los Angeles | London | New Delhi
Singapore | Washington DC

FOR INFORMATION:

SAGE Publications, Inc.
2455 Teller Road
Thousand Oaks, California 91320
E-mail: order@sagepub.com

SAGE Publications Ltd.
1 Oliver's Yard
55 City Road
London EC1Y 1SP
United Kingdom

SAGE Publications India Pvt. Ltd.
B 1/I 1 Mohan Cooperative Industrial Area
Mathura Road, New Delhi 110 044
India

SAGE Publications Asia-Pacific Pte. Ltd.
33 Pekin Street #02-01
Far East Square
Singapore 048763

Acquisitions Editor:   Vicki Knight
Associate Editor:   Lauren Habib
Editorial Assistant:   Kalie Koscielak
Production Editor:   Brittany Bauhaus
Copy Editors:   Megan Markanich, Teresa Herlinger
Typesetter:   C&M Digitals (P) Ltd.
Proofreader:   Sarah J. Duffy
Indexer:   Kathleen Paparchontis
Cover Designer:   Bryan Fishman
Permissions Editor: Adele Hutchinson

Printed in the United States of America

*Library of Congress Cataloging-in-Publication Data*

Ravitch, Sharon M.

Reason & rigor : how conceptual frameworks guide research / Sharon M. Ravitch and Matthew Riggan.

p. cm.
Includes bibliographical references and index.

ISBN 978-1-4129-8125-5 (pbk.)

1. Social sciences—Research—Methodology. 2. Research—Methodology. 3. Qualitative research. I. Riggan, Matthew. II. Title. III. Title: Reason and rigor.

H62.R344 2012
001.4'2—dc23        2011025968

This book is printed on acid-free paper.

13 14 15 10 9 8 7 6 5 4 3 2

# BRIEF CONTENTS

# DETAILED CONTENTS

# FOREWORD

One of the most difficult issues that students (and even more advanced researchers) in the social sciences, and in applied disciplines such as education, face is how to develop and use what is variously called a "conceptual framework," "theory," or "literature review." Howard Becker, in his book *Writing for Social Scientists,* has trenchantly analyzed this problem in a chapter appropriately titled "Terrorized by the Literature." Many of the dissertation proposals, and journal papers and book manuscripts, that I have reviewed lack a clear, integrated, and relevant framework of ideas that explains the authors' understanding of the topic or problem they are studying and its importance, and justifies how they are approaching it. There has been little detailed, specific guidance, in print or on the Internet, on how to create such a framework and to use it effectively in planning and conducting your research.

Sharon Ravitch and Matt Riggan have now provided an excellent practical guide for developing this framework. They define "conceptual framework" broadly, including not only the relevant theoretical literature, but also the empirical findings of prior research and the researcher's own experiential knowledge, beliefs, commitments, and values. In working through four specific examples of social research in detail, elucidating the theoretical, empirical, and personal components that framed and guided each study, they enable the reader to see what the functions of a conceptual framework are and how to begin to develop a conceptual framework for their own research.

There are several aspects of Ravitch's and Riggan's approach that I want to comment on. First, they see a conceptual framework as something that you create from multiple sources, not something that you find readymade in "the literature" and simply adopt. Existing, explicitly formulated theories can be a major source of what Becker calls the "modules" from which you develop your conceptual framework, and may provide the basic ideas and structure for this framework, but they rarely constitute the entire framework. A common problem in dissertations and published research is that the authors force their data to fit a single theory, ignoring places where this theory distorts or ignores important aspects of the problem or phenomenon studied (Dressman, 2008). Reality is always more complex than any theory can completely capture, and you need to construct a conceptual framework that takes account of this complexity and avoids gross oversimplifications of the things you are studying, as best you can.

In my view, your conceptual framework is a lens, or better, a set of lenses, for making sense of these things, and often is most useful when it incorporates complementary theories that capture different aspects of your subject. Jennifer Greene, in her book *Mixed Methods in Social Inquiry,* refers to this as a dialectic stance for research, recognizing that different philosophical, theoretical, and methodological approaches have different strengths and limitations, and that it is often most productive to try to engage these different approaches with one another, in ways that provide generative insights and a deeper understanding than any single theory or approach can provide.

Second, your conceptual framework is not simply an assortment of ideas and theoretical modules. The pieces should relate to one another in some way, to exhibit some sort of coherence; this is part of what Ravitch and Riggan mean by describing a conceptual framework as an "argument." This doesn't have to be a strict logical consistency; as stated above, it is often valuable to incorporate diverse, and even apparently contradictory, ideas in your conceptual framework. However, it does mean that you need to think about *how* the different pieces relate to one another, and what aspects of your subject each is most valuable for understanding. You also need to effectively communicate to your readers how this particular integration of ideas seems to you to provide the best approach for your research, and how it informs your research questions and methodological decisions.

Finally, your conceptual framework is not something that you construct before beginning your research and then leave unchanged, as a fixed "foundation" for your methods and analysis. This framework needs to be responsive to what you are learning from your research experiences and data; the latter will often necessitate additions or modifications to this framework, or even creating a substantial part of this framework through the generation of "grounded theory" from the data. A conceptual framework is not simply a visual or verbal *presentation* of your ideas; it is the *actual* framework of ideas and commitments that are informing and guiding your study, and may require ongoing reflection in order for you to fully understand these (Maxwell, in press).

In clear prose and with numerous examples and questions, Ravitch and Riggan shepherd their readers through the challenging process of understanding, creating, and using conceptual frameworks for their research. I don't know of a better guide for this process.

—*Joseph Maxwell*

# PREFACE

In our work with graduate students over the years, we have watched many struggle mightily with the challenge of arguing for (that is, being able to articulate the reasons for and goals of) their study topics and methods. Some students come to us with what they believe to be fully formed research questions and designs, but have been told (usually by their dissertation chair) that their study lacks a "theoretical framework," effectively sending them back to the library in search of one. Others have received the vague suggestion that their dissertation needs "more of a literature review," which is rather like telling a culinary student that their soup needs "more ingredients." Still others present us with "conceptual frameworks" represented by elegant flowcharts but divorced from their discussion of the literature or their research methods. The common factor in most of these scenarios is a troubling disconnect between what students are reading about their topics, their thinking about what research questions matter and why, and their strategies for exploring those questions. This set of disconnects often results in ongoing frustration for both students and those who advise them. All too often this leads to studies like those described above—diligently executed but, in critical respects, underconceptualized. The implications of this conceptual weakness for the quality of the studies' research designs (and the resulting empirical work itself) cannot be overestimated.

This book presents *conceptual frameworks* as a mechanism—process and product—for resolving much of this confusion and lack of coherence. We define a conceptual framework as *an argument about why the topic one wishes to study matters, and why the means proposed to study it are appropriate and rigorous* (a more comprehensive definition appears in the next chapter). In this sense, the conceptual framework is both a guide and a ballast for empirical research, situating specific questions and strategies for exploring them within the wider universe of what is already known about a given topic or question. A conceptual framework allows researchers to make reasoned, defensible choices about how we might explore topics or themes heretofore underexplored or to explore old questions in new contexts. It matches our research questions with those choices, and in turn aligns our analytic tools and methods with our questions. It also guides the ways in which we think about collecting, analyzing, describing, and interpreting our data. This book seeks to make these concepts, as well as the processes of developing and defining conceptual frameworks, clear and accessible to the reader.

Conceptual frameworks (or aspects of conceptual frameworks such as literature reviews or theoretical frameworks) are often presented to students as a requirement for scholarly work with little explanation of why they are important and even less guidance about their direct, iterative role in the development and implementation of empirical research. As a result, many students end up citing theory that is not connected to their data collection or analysis or presenting their reader with "laundry list" literature reviews—extensive discussions of everything that has ever been written about a given topic with little or no sense of why it is important to know or how the literatures fit together.

*Reason and Rigor* aims to help students and other researchers understand the functional, comprehensive role of conceptual frameworks in organizing and guiding their empirical research. We view the development of conceptual frameworks as a process through which researchers identify the questions and lines of inquiry that matter most to them, develop appropriate strategies for pursuing those questions, and monitor and reflect on their own learning and thinking as the research unfolds. As a result, readers of this book will learn how to *use* existing knowledge (theory, methods, and empirical research) in conjunction with their own interests and observations to ask better questions, develop robust and justifiable strategies for exploring those questions, and explain both the importance and limitations of their findings.

## ☆ ORGANIZATION OF THIS BOOK

In the opening chapter of this book, we briefly summarize the function of a conceptual framework and delve more deeply into defining it, describing its primary elements such as theory, methodology, and literature review. In Chapter 2 *Why Conceptual Frameworks?* we outline our argument for why this book is needed. Specifically, we focus on a troubling lack of clarity about the meaning and role of theory and about the purpose and function of literature review. We also discuss what we view as the impenetrability and opacity of the research process as a context for the importance of understanding the central role of conceptual frameworks in empirical research.

In Chapter 3, *Excavating Questions: Conceptual Frameworks* and *Research Design*, we analyze the mixed methods research of James Spillane, a widely recognized researcher in the educational policy arena, on how school district officials think about teacher learning. We show how Spillane's argument for the importance of his topic shaped decisions about the type of data needed and strategies for collecting and analyzing those data. We also highlight the iterative and evolving nature of both conceptual frameworks and research designs by showing how Spillane's conceptual framework grew out of what he had already learned from previous analyses.

In Chapter 4, *The Role of the Conceptual Framework in Data Collection and Fieldwork*, we engage with the research of Michelle Fine, a widely recognized qualitative researcher who specializes in participatory action research and other applied qualitative methodologies that sit at the intersection of psychology, education, and sociology. After contextualizing her work in general terms, we use her study of Muslim youth in politically contentious contexts to focus on the role of conceptual frameworks in the data collection and fieldwork more broadly. We focus specifically on how the conceptual framework for this research was developed and its relationship to a series of interrelated methodological choices about research design with a focus on data collection. This includes a discussion of how the conceptual framework influenced decisions about site selection, sampling, and sequencing of methods, including the development of instruments and the process of examining the role and identity of the researcher and its impact on methodological stance and methods choices.

Chapter 5, *Conceptual Frameworks and the Analysis of Data,* highlights the work of Frederick Erickson, an educational anthropologist who has helped shape the field of qualitative educational research. In this chapter we explore data analysis as a series of decisions about how a researcher interacts with the data and explicate how conceptual frameworks inform and guide the recursive process of framing for data analysis. We specifically examine how conceptual frameworks inform data analysis in terms of the researcher's choices of analytic themes and categories as well as specific methodological choices such as transcription, coding, and data display. Erickson's work provides an instructive example of the role of conceptual frameworks in guiding both the organization and interpretation of data and, in so doing, clarifies and explains the powerful role of the conceptual framework across each stage of the data analysis process.

Chapter 6, *Expanding the Conversation, Extending the Argument: The Role of Conceptual Frameworks in Presenting, Explaining, and Contextualizing Findings,* focuses on the work of Margaret Beale Spencer in developing a phenomenological variant on ecological systems theory (PVEST). The chapter highlights the relationship between theoretical frameworks (of which PVEST is an excellent example) and the wider conceptual frameworks within which they are situated. This chapter also highlights the ways in which researchers use conceptual frameworks to integrate and interpret findings that align with and extend the theory we develop and use, as well as what we do when findings appear contrary to our expectations.

Chapter 7, *The Conceptual Framework as Guide and Ballast,* looks across chapters to make an argument about the value and importance of the conceptual framework in empirical research as well as about its role in shaping study design and implementation. In this chapter, we examine the role of conceptual frameworks as both guide and ballast, describing how they serve to help researchers chart a course, design studies, make informed methodological choices, and ground their emerging understandings and interpretations. After revisiting our working definition of a conceptual framework, we offer readers ideas for how to approach the kind of ongoing reflexive engagement—conceptually and methodologically—that solid empirical research requires. We offer guided exercises such as prompted research exercises, concept maps, research memos, and the ongoing writing (and rereading) of a research journal to support researchers in the process of developing your own conceptual frameworks.

Within and across chapters, the book seeks to clarify and explicate the complicated and multifaceted role of conceptual frameworks in such a way as to enrich your understanding of their roles and uses as well as to help you as a researcher embark on the development and refinement of conceptual frameworks in your own research.

## ☆ ACKNOWLEDGMENTS

We wish to jointly express our thanks:

To the authors whose work we focus on—Frederick Erickson, Michelle Fine, Margaret Beale Spencer, and Jim Spillane—for your good and important work in the world, for helping us to learn about and understand the value and uses of conceptual frameworks, and for your wonderful collaboration throughout the writing of this book. You have left large footsteps for generations of researchers to fill. We are grateful.

To our editor, Vicki Knight, for your thoughtful assistance in all stages of this work, for your belief in the value of this book, and for your ongoing support.

To Joseph Maxwell, mentor and colleague. You are a north for generations of researchers. Thank you for teaching us across the years and for teaching our students through your excellent works in the area of qualitative research and theory more broadly.

To Ginger Stull and Aaron Weiss for your significant help with transcription, permissions, editing, and logistics. Special thanks to Corrie Tice for your help and overall support with the book. Thank you to Maureen Cotterill and Vernell Edwards for your ongoing support.

We wish to express our appreciation to our reviewers for their thoughtful feedback and constructive suggestions on various iterations of this book. Thank you to Kathleen Gershman *(University of North Dakota)*, Kyle Greenwalt *(Michigan State University)*, Mark Moritz *(The Ohio State University)*, Leslie Nabors Olah *(School District of Philadelphia)*, Cleti Cervoni *(Salem State University)*, and Catherine Belcher *(LA's Promise)* for your support of our work.

Sharon wishes to thank:

My early and ongoing mentors, Fred Erickson, Carol Gilligan, Sara Lawrence-Lightfoot, Michael Nakkula, Kathy Schultz, and Joseph Maxwell, for helping me to cultivate myself as a researcher, thinker, and doer.

My wonderful, supportive colleagues at The University of Pennsylvania Graduate School of Education with whom I conduct and teach research: Susan Lytle, Peter Kuriloff, Mike Johanek, Susan Yoon, Elliot Weinbaum, Janine Remillard, Howard Stevenson, Jon Supovitz, Henry May, Torch Lytle, Dana Kaminstein, and Doug Lynch for your colleagueship, your influence, and your friendship. Dean Andy Porter, for your ongoing support of my work and specifically my international research. A special thank you to Matthew Riggan, my coauthor, coteacher, and cothinker; you are a teacher and researcher par excellence (and a truly gifted writer!).

Generations of students with whom I have engaged in research, you have also been my teachers: Matthew Tarditi, for being my research partner, teacher, and kindred spirit in our ongoing research in Nicaragua; Gabriel Dattatreyan and Arjun Shankar, for being thought partners in the truest sense and for building together our important research in India; Laura Colket, for being my right-hand woman in our applied development research work in Haiti; Shannon Andrus, for your energy, thoughtfulness, and rigor in our school-based participatory research; Chris Steel, for engaging with me in research in Latin America that works toward *el bien comun*, Sarah Klevan, Ellie Fitts-Fulmer, Brian Girard, and Reed Roeser, for helping me think through issues related to research and critical pedagogy; Kathleen Wirth, for helping me to understand the ins and outs of insider action research in schools; Heather Curl, for your energy, commitment, and vision in our work in the Inter-American Leadership Network; John Baker, Jeremy Cutler, Tanya Maloney, Brandon Miller, Joseph Nelson, Chris Pupik-Dean, and Amanda Soto, for your commitment to participatory research in schools through your dedicated work at the Center for the Study of Boys' and Girls' Lives. To my teaching assistants who have helped me to consider what teaching research really means and entails: Christa Bialka, Sue Bickerstaff, Carolyn Chernoff, Jaskiran Dhillon, Danielle Gioia, Chike McLoyd, Carolyn McGuire, Stacie Molnar-Main, Kathleen Riley, Jamey Rorison, Sonia Rosen, Susan Thomas, and Kelly Wissman. To the students of the Mid-Career Doctoral Program in Educational Leadership and the CLO Doctoral Program, who have individually and collectively provided a community in which to see and understand the complexities and uses of, as well as the need for, local knowledge construction through practitioner research.

My international research colleagues with whom I learn about the contextual, and particularly the sociopolitical, variables that shape and influence applied educational development research. My dear colleagues in Nicaragua: the Baltodano family (Duilio, Ernesto, Dania, and Indiana), Adriana Chamorro, Eveling Estrada, the CISA Exportadora and CISA Agro staff, Felipe Perez and Arkangel Cordero of Instituto Centroamericano de Administración de Empresas (INCAE Business School), the great minds and hearts of Generation Atlas (especially Ernesto Baltodano, Kenneth Urbina, and Paccelly Torres), Kevin Maranacci of the Fabretto Foundation, and Carlos Briceno. My colleagues in Ecuador: Helen and Eugenio Braun, Graciela Castelo, Sam DuBois (*mi voz*), and the staff and incredible students at the Centro Integral de la Familia. My new and esteemed colleagues in Haiti: Creutzer Mathurin, Sergot Jacob, Jacky Lumarque, and Carole Sassine. And in India: Gauri Bhure, Gowri Ishrawan, E. S. Ramamurthy, and the leadership team at the Azim Premji Foundation. My colleagues in the United States who help me to conceptualize my applied research work: the brilliant, patient, endlessly energetic and generous David Land (words are inadequate), Michael Reichert (dear friend, mentor, and thought partner), Yve-Car Momperousse, Cathi Tilman, Brett Stoudt, and Theodore Burnes. And a major thank-you to the many school and community members across the globe who have opened your homes, schools, and communities to me and have taught me so much about the true meaning of strength and generosity.

To my family: My husband, Andy, and my sons, Ari and Lev, for supporting me, inspiring me, grounding me, and cheering me on. My parents, Arline and Carl Ravitch, for your incredible support, faith, and enduring generosity of spirit. Sheila and Larry Burstein, Gary and Mindy Karp, and my siblings: Frank and Jamie Ravitch, Elizabeth and Auren Weinberg, Evan and Randi Burstein, and Peter and Wendy Burstein, for all of your support, encouragement, and love. To my community of friends: Deborah Melincoff, Laura Hoffman, Jennifer and Michael Finkelstein, Peter Siskind, Stefanie Gabel, Amy Leventhal, Alyssa Levy, Wendy McGrath, Jenny and Michael Raphael, Heather and Joel DeGrands, Shari Short, Aaron Toffler, Gabrielle Kaplan-Mayer, and Christina Ager. Thank you for sustaining me.

Matt wishes to thank:

First and foremost, I need to thank Sharon for being such a thoughtful and energetic partner and coauthor. I have learned so much from this experience. You are a pleasure to work with.

Thanks to my research and teaching colleagues at Penn: Jonathan Supovitz, Elliot Weinbaum, Henry May, Leslie Nabors Oláh, Andrea Oettinger, Torch Lytle, Mike Johanek, Kathleen Hall, Ira Harkavy (who more than anyone taught me the importance of argument), and Cory Bowman. I am lucky to have such conscientious and gifted colleagues with whom I can muddle through the questions and problems we confront in our work. Thanks also to Doug Lynch and Stanton Wortham for giving me the opportunity to teach and work with graduate students, without which this book would not exist.

Since the beginning of graduate school, two close friends, Cathy Belcher and Aiden Downey, have been consistent sounding boards and thought partners in virtually every intellectual endeavor I have undertaken. Your companionship and insight (along with your humor and irreverence) have been as important to my learning as anything else I've been up to these last ten years.

None of this means much without family. To my wife Erin, thank you for all of your support, for sharing in my nerdy enthusiasm for this project, and for the sacrifices you made to allow me to pursue this project. To my sons Ian and Miles, thanks for tolerating all of the times Daddy was chained to the computer. I'll have more play time now, I promise. To my parents, John and Ann, my sister Jennifer (a brilliant scholar in her own right) and brother-in-law Ermias, and to Francis Vargas and Kim Katz, thanks for being all that a family should be. Your love and support make possible things far more consequential than this book, but this book would not be possible without them.

# ABOUT THE AUTHORS

**Sharon M. Ravitch, PhD,** is a senior lecturer at the University of Pennsylvania's Graduate School of Education. Ravitch's research integrates across the fields of qualitative research, education, applied development, cultural anthropology, and human development and has three main strands: (1) practitioner research as a means of engendering professional and institutional development; (2) international applied educational development research that works from a participatory approach (research projects are currently in Nicaragua, Haiti, India, and Ecuador); and (3) ethnography within and across disciplines. She has published three earlier books: *Metodología de la Investigación Cualitativa* (Qualitative Research Methods: A Reader), *School Counseling Principles: Diversity and Multiculturalism*, and *Matters of Interpretation: Reciprocal Transformation in Therapeutic and Developmental Relationships With Youth* (With Michael Nakkula). Ravitch is the newly appointed senior international advisor to the Haitian Ministry of Education for their Educational Reconstruction Plan. She is research co-director at the Center for the Study of Boys' and Girls' Lives. She holds two master's degrees from Harvard University and a doctorate from the University of Pennsylvania.

**Matthew Riggan, PhD,** is a senior researcher at the Consortium for Policy Research in Education at the University of Pennsylvania and an adjunct assistant professor in Penn's Graduate School of Education. His current research focuses on formative assessment in elementary mathematics; assessing analytic and problem-solving skills for postsecondary readiness; systemic reform to support science, technology, engineering, and mathematics (STEM) education; and factors supporting or undermining the expansion and institutionalization of promising reforms in urban school districts. He teaches courses in qualitative research design, data collection, and analysis, and has worked extensively on developing qualitative and mixed methods approaches to program theory evaluation and analysis of video data. He holds a doctorate in anthropology and education from the University of Pennsylvania.

# CHAPTER 1

# INTRODUCTION

I magine for a moment that you are an archaeologist interested in the number systems employed by pre-Colombian civilizations in Mexico and Central America. Where your interest in this specific topic comes from may be hard to pinpoint. Maybe it's the idea that there was some system in place before the numbers we use today, which we have a hard time seeing as but one of many possible systems for counting things. Perhaps it's a desire to better understand the intellectual achievements of civilizations long slighted by Western historians. Maybe as a child growing up in Mexico you long wondered about the origins of the math curricula that guided your learning in school. Perhaps you were a Peace Corps volunteer in Mexico and have become interested in local knowledge construction. Maybe you came upon some rare documents that suggest earlier counting systems that have been heretofore unexplored. Whatever the prompt may be, you have your reasons for selecting this topic for your research.

But reasons are not enough. Assuming you have a basic familiarity with archaeology, you still have a raft of questions to grapple with before you can begin your research study. For starters, what data are you actually looking for? After all, you are not likely to find an old, dog-eared copy of the *Olmec Guide to Numbering and Calculation* buried next to a giant stone head. How will you find material evidence of what is basically a cognitive construct? How will you know when you have found it? What do you expect the artifacts you find to tell you about the number systems they represent? Why are they important? How do you ascertain historical context broadly and specifically in relation to the focus of your research?

Then there is the matter of where to look. Southern Mexico and Central America cover a lot of ground. On top of that, the actual borders denoted by those names are meaningless, given that they did not exist during the period you seek to study. How will you know where to begin your search?

Assuming you can somehow answer those questions, you then confront the question of how you will actually search for evidence. Who will you involve in the searching and (if you're lucky) excavation process? What kind of technology will you use? Once you have these issues covered, you will need to think about how to catalogue anything that you find. This in turn begs the question of how you will want to analyze the information you collect.

In short, you have a lot of work to do. The good news is that you have help. Many others have asked themselves questions that are similar to the ones you are now asking. They have already gone through the processes we have just outlined. And happily for you, many of them have already written about it. Some of them went about their work carefully and meticulously, while others may have been more careless. Some pioneered new methods, while others stayed within convention. Some focused on simply documenting what they found, while others sought out and tested possible explanations. Each has something important to teach you about how to approach your own study.

Some of what you read will tell you where there are known archaeological sites that may serve as a good place to begin your search. Other material may include images that you think might possibly contain evidence of number systems and therefore warrant closer examination. Still other sources may focus on entirely different civilizations or periods, but employ methods for searching, cataloguing, or analysis that seem relevant to your questions. A completely separate body of work may hint at the role of number systems in agriculture or in religious rites, methods of deduction that could prove useful.

You dive into these assorted literatures, noting the ways in which they speak to you and to each other, how they shape and refine your research questions, sharpen your focus, and give you insight into your methods. You continually reshuffle and reorganize them as you become better acquainted with their content. By the time you are finished reading, writing, and thinking about what you have learned, you have a pretty clear idea what you are looking for and why, where you want to look, how you plan to look for it, and what you will do with what you find. And while you cannot be sure what precisely that is, you have some reasoned ideas about how what you find will inform your thinking, and that of others, about this topic. You are ready to go into the field.

In working through these questions, you have constructed a *conceptual framework* for your research. You have figured out what you want to study and why it matters (to you and broader audiences), and you have arrived at reasonable conclusions about how to go about studying it (methodology). The process of building this conceptual framework began with your personal interests—without them you would not be doing the work, after all—but it was your learning beyond that first stage, or foundation, that gave shape to the research.

Okay, so you are probably not an archaeologist. Neither are we. So why use this analogy?

When we frame the need for learning in material terms—needing to know what to look for and where to look for it—it seems obvious that we would use the collective expertise of others to help us make good choices about how to go about framing, structuring, and approaching our research studies. It seems equally apparent that having engaged in this process of learning about prior research that relates to and informs our own research, we should articulate a clear rationale for how we frame and approach our own research to someone who is new to our work.

By contrast, most social science research is not concerned with the physical search for material things. Consequently, it becomes easy to lose sight of the need for a systematic way of thinking through and articulating what you plan to study and how you plan to study it. For many researchers, personal interest, topic, research questions, literature, and methods seem to drift away from one another, taking their studies with them, leaving the research underconceptualized and methodologically hazy.

As teachers and advisors to graduate students, we encounter this problem all the time. One of our students (let's call him Chris) crafted an entire draft of his dissertation proposal only to be told by his advisor that he needed a theoretical framework. He was not told why or for what purpose. An even less lucky student, Arjun, was keenly interested in a specific topic and was told by his advisor which theoretical framework to use, but after reading a dozen or so articles could not figure out how the theory fit with his topic or research setting. Jayla had more luck linking topic and theory, but her design faltered methodologically. She intended to use surveys to link attitudes, behaviors, and outcomes, but her questions were all interpretive. By contrast, Angela proposed a qualitative interview study paired with observation notes, but made no argument whatsoever for why such data collection strategies were appropriate to or necessary for her topic.

Failure to conceptualize and articulate these connections as the bedrock of a solid empirical study undermines your research in at least three ways. First, it makes your work conceptually murky. Researchers often explain, for example, that their work is "informed by" some line of theory, but fail to explain the specific ways that these theories bear on their own conceptualizations.

Second, a weak conceptual framework leads to weak methodological arguments. Often, it seems as if the methodology of a study is preordained by the field in which it is conducted, irrespective of the topic. It is of little surprise, then, that arguments for the relevance of a topic (why it is worth studying) are silent on methods (how it should be studied). Third, it can leave you adrift in your empirical work. Rather than make their own argument for why their work matters, novice researchers often find themselves in the unenviable position of trying to associate their work with a raft of different theoretical approaches simply because those approaches have previously been used to study their topic. When confronted with ambiguity, complexity, or change in the course of their work, they are often unable to fall back on a coherent rationale for the choices they have made, and thus have no basis to make good decisions about how to modify or adjust their methods and frameworks as the study unfolds.

Using examples from multiple research topics that work within and across disciplines, this book shows—in broad and specific ways—how developing a sturdy conceptual framework can help you to circumvent or work through these common challenges. We argue that a conceptual framework both shapes the design and direction of your study and guides its evolution. Analyzing four existing research studies to unpack and explore the roles and uses of conceptual frameworks, we show how what you learn in the field in turn feeds back into your conceptual framework, allowing you to integrate it into your overall understanding of the topic, research methods, and presentation of findings.

As with most useful books related to methodology, we ground our discussion of conceptual frameworks in real examples from the literature rather than discussing them in the abstract. Thankfully, robust conceptual frameworks and strong arguments are relatively easy to find. What is missing is an explanation of what *makes* a framework robust or an argument strong. Our aim in this book is to draw out and employ lessons from exemplary research so that you can use them in your own work. In the chapters that follow, we present and analyze the conceptual frameworks of four published works by a highly accomplished and diverse group of scholars, paired with reflection and commentary of the authors of those works that were garnered through one-on-one interviews that focused on the role of the study's conceptual framework in various aspects and stages of their research. The book is organized to explore, through the focused examination of these four studies, the role of conceptual frameworks within and across the goals and stages of conducting an empirical study. Specifically, we examine the impact of the authors' conceptual frameworks on four major stages of the research process: research questions and design, data collection and fieldwork, data analysis, and presentation of findings.

Beyond their ability to articulate a clear and compelling rationale for their research, we chose the specific authors and studies featured in this book for several reasons. First, the four authors represent a diversity of disciplinary backgrounds. James Spillane, whose work is featured in Chapter 3, is a policy researcher interested in the dynamics of organizational change. Michelle Fine's work (Chapter 4) falls primarily into the category of participatory research and focuses on questions of identity, agency, and power among marginalized populations. In Chapter 5 we highlight the research of educational anthropologist Frederick Erickson, whose work seeks to understand how communication and interaction work in various settings, including schools. Margaret Beale Spencer's social psychology research (Chapter 6) examines the range of home, school, and community factors that influence the capacity of young people to cope with the challenges of race and social class inequality.

Second, while all four of the scholars whose work is in focus in this book have conducted research that relates in some way to schools or education, the focus of the four articles discussed here reaches well beyond that particular field. Spillane's article falls squarely within the realm of educational research, focusing on school reform implementation. In the other three articles, however, schooling is more the backdrop than the focal point. Both Fine and Spencer's articles focus on identity construction, though they do so in vastly different ways, and Erickson's article primarily analyzes the underlying structure and timing of communication. Overall, the range of topics and questions explored in these articles should be of interest to audiences well outside of the field of education.

Finally, we deliberately chose scholars and articles whose work represents a range of methodological approaches. Among the four articles featured here, one (Spencer) utilizes quantitative methods exclusively, while another (Fine) uses quantitative methods alongside qualitative approaches (what is commonly referred to as "mixed methods research") from the fields of psychology and anthropology. The remaining two articles are qualitative, but in quite different ways. Spillane's article utilizes classroom observations and interviews to better understand broad concepts, while Erickson employs fine-grained analyses of interaction common in sociolinguistics.

In sum, we selected the scholars and articles for this book with an eye toward making its central themes as broadly applicable across topics and disciplines as possible. This is not a book about how to do research—you will not find much discussion of the nuts and bolts of constructing interview protocols, creating analysis categories, designing surveys, or choosing appropriate statistical techniques. There are already plenty of good resources focused on those topics. What this book focuses on is how to make informed, sophisticated choices about engaging in each and all of these aspects of empirical research, how to justify and explain your research choices to your audiences, and how to integrate what you learn from your empirical work with what you already know.

In the remainder of this chapter, we present our definition of a conceptual framework, comparing and contrasting our definition with those employed by other scholars. We then explain what informs the development of a conceptual framework, including your personal interests and values, existing research on the topic of interest, and theoretical frameworks. We emphasize that while a conceptual framework is an argument for a study's topic and methods, implicit within that argument are decisions and assumptions about the researcher's relationship to the topic and setting. We conclude the chapter with a discussion of how conceptual frameworks shape (and are shaped by) different aspects of the research process: research design, data collection and fieldwork, data analysis, and presentation and contextualization of findings.

## ☆ CONCEPTUAL FRAMEWORKS EXPLORED AND DEFINED

In our many conversations with colleagues and students, we have found that the term *conceptual framework* is used to refer to at least three different things. Some view it as a purely visual representation of a study's organization or major theoretical tenets. Such a representation is usually included within one's literature review, generally as a stand-alone figure.

A second perspective treats conceptual and theoretical frameworks as essentially the same thing. As with theoretical frameworks, the meaning of *conceptual frameworks* in this sense depends entirely on what one means by *theory*. As we argue in the next chapter, a problem can arise when researchers are vague about such definitions, as conceptual/theoretical frameworks in this sense can refer to either "off the shelf" (existing) or "homegrown" (your own integration of concepts) theories.

A third view sees the conceptual framework as a way of linking all of the elements of the research process: researcher disposition, interest, and positionality; literature; and theory and methods. It is this view that comes closest to our own definition. In the sections below, we offer our own definition of the term, explain how we arrived at that definition, and describe in detail how conceptual frameworks are related to other critical components of the research process, such as theory and literature review. In the process, we offer our own working definitions of those components as well. Our aim in defining our terms is not to engage in semantic debates with other scholars. (Truth be told, we are not concerned with what you call it. As with defining analytic themes or codes in qualitative research, the definition is far more important than the label!) Rather, our hope is that we can be clear and transparent about how we are employing specific terms. As Chapter 2 shows, part of the reason why there is so much confusion about this topic is the careless way in which many scholars define and employ terms. We have no desire to compound this problem.

For us, a conceptual framework is an argument about why the topic one wishes to study matters, and why the means proposed to study it are appropriate and rigorous. By *argument*, we mean that a conceptual framework is a series of sequenced, logical propositions the purpose of which is to convince the reader of the study's importance and rigor. Arguments for why a study "matters" vary greatly in scale, depending on the audience. In some scholarly work, the study may only matter to a small, esoteric community, but that does not change the fact that its conceptual framework should argue for its relevance within that community. Finally, by *appropriate and rigorous*, we mean that a conceptual framework should argue convincingly that (1) the research questions are an outgrowth of the argument for relevance; (2) the data to be collected provide the researcher with the raw material needed to explore the research questions; and (3) the analytic approach allows the researcher to effectively respond to (if not always answer) those questions. Further, rigor includes not only how a study is carried out, but also how the methodology itself is conceptualized. As we will see in Chapter 4 and Chapter 5 in particular, methodology is neither objective nor value-neutral. As such, what you study and how you study it ultimately raises questions about who you are, what kinds of questions you ask, the assumptions embedded within those questions, and the extent to which those assumptions are made explicit and, where appropriate, subjected to critique.

While our definition of a conceptual framework is different from others, the ideas behind that definition are not new. In their popular and enduring book *Qualitative Data Analysis*, Miles and Huberman (1994) argue that novice researchers should spend considerable time at the outset of their research conceptualizing, identifying the components of, and articulating (often in graphic as well as narrative form) their conceptual framework. They assert that the building of theory relies on central, broad constructs or categories, which they refer to as *intellectual bins*, that contain multiple, discrete events and behaviors (p. 18). They argue that "setting out bins, naming them, and getting clearer about their interrelationships" leads the researcher to his or her conceptual framework. They further assert that the conceptual framework is central to this intellectual sorting work, which they refer to as "the focusing and bounding function of a conceptual framework" (p. 19). Developing a conceptual framework forces the researcher to be selective, to prioritize variables, and to discern specific relationships within the research. Miles and Huberman define a conceptual framework in this way:

> A conceptual framework explains, either graphically or in narrative form, the main things to be studied—the key factors, constructs or variables—and the presumed relationships among them. Frameworks can be rudimentary or elaborate, theory-driven or commonsensical, descriptive or causal. (p. 18)

In *Qualitative Research Design: An Interactive Approach*, Maxwell (2005) devotes an entire chapter to conceptual frameworks (in the 1996 first edition this was called *conceptual context*). Maxwell defines a conceptual framework in this way: "The conceptual framework of your study [is] the system of concepts, assumptions, expectations, beliefs, and theories that supports and informs your research. [It] is a key part of your design" (p. 33). Building on Miles and Huberman's (1994) definition, Maxwell asserts that he uses the term *conceptual framework* "in a broader sense that includes the actual ideas and beliefs that you hold about the phenomena studied, whether these are written down or not" (p. 33).

Maxwell (2005) makes the important argument that the "conceptual framework of your research study is something that is *constructed*, not found. It incorporates pieces that are borrowed from elsewhere, but the structure, the overall coherence, is something that *you* build, not something that exists ready-made" (p. 35). He describes the conceptual framework as a combination of experiential knowledge and prior theory and research. Maxwell makes the argument that a conceptual framework is a theory, albeit at times a tentative or partial one. He contends that one might even use terms like *theoretical framework* or *idea context* rather than *conceptual framework*. While we depart from him in this latter issue of naming (we see the theoretical framework, as we will discuss below, as a component of a conceptual framework) we agree with him substantively on the frames, roles, and uses of the idea of a conceptual framework.

While they do not define the term specifically, in *Designing Qualitative Research* Marshall and Rossman (2006) spend a chapter focusing on conceptual frameworks, offering a different view of their content and purpose. In their view, the conceptual framework has two primary elements. First, it as an argument for the study's significance:

> Convincing a reader that the study is significant and should be conducted entails building an argument that links research to important theoretical perspectives, policy issues, concerns of practice, or social issues that affect people's everyday lives. (pp. 33–34)

Second, Marshall and Rossman (2006) suggest that the conceptual framework reflects "the important intellectual traditions that guide the study" (p. 26). They further note that these traditions are identified through a careful and thorough review of literature related to the study's topic.

In addition to explaining what a conceptual framework is, these authors offer some useful ideas about its purpose and function. Miles and Huberman (1994) note the importance of conceptual frameworks as a learning tool. They stress that while conceptual frameworks help to organize your work, they are also malleable, evolving over time as the various relevant entities and relationships become more clearly discernable.

> As qualitative researchers collect data, they revise their frameworks—make them more precise, replace empirically feeble bins with more meaningful ones, and reconstrue relationships. Conceptual frameworks are simply the current version of the researchers' map of the territory being investigated. As the explorer's knowledge of the terrain improves, the map becomes correspondingly more differentiated and integrated, and researchers . . . can coordinate their data collection even more closely. (p. 20)

This view of the conceptual framework as a guide and ballast in research, while at the same time evolving as the research develops, reflects a perspective that we share and will build on throughout this book. This conception of the need for rigor and fluidity in a conceptual framework has more recently been echoed by an emphasis on the conceptual framework as an organizing, if transitional, force in empirical research (Leshem, 2007; Morse, 2004).

Maxwell (2005), whose work has influenced generations of qualitative and mixed methods researchers, makes a critical point about the importance of conceptual frameworks in clarifying, explaining, and justifying method-ological decisions.

> The most important thing to understand about your conceptual framework is that it is primarily a conception or model of what is out there that you plan to study, and of what is going on with these things and why—a tentative *theory* of the phenomena that you are investigating. The function of this theory is to inform the rest of your design—to help you to assess and refine your goals, develop realistic and relevant research questions, select appropriate methods, and identify potential validity threats to your conclusions. It also helps you *justify* your research. (pp. 33–34)

Our definition of a conceptual framework draws from each of these conceptualizations. From Miles and Huberman (1994) and from Maxwell (2005), we incorporate the idea that conceptual frameworks seek to identify "presumed relationships" among key factors or constructs to be studied, and that the justification for these presumptions may come from multiple sources such as one's own prior research or "tentative theories" as well as established theoretical or empirical work found in the research literature. We strongly agree with Maxwell's observation that through the process of developing a conceptual framework, the researcher comes to take ownership of the study's core concepts and logic, a point that fits nicely with Miles and Huberman's view of the conceptual framework as both a tool for and artifact of the researcher's learning. From Marshall and Rossman (2006), we adopt the explicit view of the conceptual framework as an argument for the study's importance, a stance echoed by Maxwell's view of the conceptual framework as "justifying" the research both substantively and methodologically.

Where we depart somewhat from these characterizations of conceptual frameworks is in the degree to which we seek to define and clarify the relationship between the conceptual framework and what we view as its component parts. For instance, Miles and Huberman (1994) indicate that conceptual frameworks may be comprised of formal theories, observations, hunches, personal interests, or hypotheses, but say little about how these very different types of knowledge or inference fit together. Maxwell (2005) uses the terms *conceptual framework* and *theoretical framework* interchangeably, while Marshall and Rossman (2006) conflate conceptual frameworks with literature reviews. As we argue in the next chapter, this vagueness, combined with the multiple, idiosyncratic meanings ascribed to these terms, contributes greatly to the confusion about the role that these component parts play in guiding research.

In our view, conceptual frameworks are comprised of three primary elements: personal interests, topical research, and theoretical frameworks. Though it is often described as a product, we view literature review first and foremost as a process through which conceptual frameworks are developed.

*Personal interests* include your own curiosities, biases, and ideological commitments (what you think is interesting or important), theories of action (why you think things happen), and epistemological assumptions (what constitutes useful or valuable knowledge), all of which are profoundly influenced by your social location (race, ethnicity, social class, gender, sexual identification, nationality, and other social identities), institutional position, and life experience. As we explore in Chapter 4, what this means is that any inquiry into what you study also requires some reflection on who you are, since that in turn informs (and biases) your perception of things. For example, an extensive critique of early (and in some cases more current) ethnographic research shows how the interpretation of observed behaviors is profoundly influenced by the cultural values of the observer (Fordham, 1996). In quantitative research, questions have been raised about the assumptions of race neutrality that frequently accompany experimental designs. Strict adherence to method is viewed as a check on racial and other forms of bias. Yet there is reason to wonder whether the race of the researcher affects the findings of experimental studies even when methodology is held constant (Goar, 2008). This does not mean that certain topics should be off limits to certain researchers, but it does mean that personal background, professional role, and social location need to be viewed as methodological considerations worthy of critical attention.

Beyond individual characteristics such as race, ethnicity, or language, your position in relation to the research setting is a critical consideration. In practitioner research, for example, what constitutes an important research question might have less to do with the state of the literature on a given topic and more to do with pressing concerns of the practitioner herself given the issues or problems of practice from which the questions emerge. In traditions such as participatory action research, the framing of research questions is itself a process of figuring out what type of knowledge is valuable in a given setting or community (Greenwood & Levin, 1998).

Personal interests are what drive you to do the work in the first place—your motivation for asking questions and seeking knowledge. As such, they play an important role in the process of conceptualizing and carrying out empirical research. However, they are merely a first step in doing so. Belief alone is not evidence. Interest alone is not an argument for why a study matters. Hunches about how the world works do not constitute a theoretical framework.

As you review the literature related to a given topic, your personal interests evolve into conceptual frameworks. Literature review allows you to survey what is known about a given topic, how that topic has been investigated, and the intellectual and analytic tools that might help you to understand it better. As a researcher, you must critically read and make connections between, or integrate and synthesize, existing work related to your emerging research topic and its multiple theoretical and practical contexts. As suggested by Maxwell (2010), this process frequently calls for critiques of existing theoretical or empirical work, as well as of your own biases or assumptions. A skeptical eye is needed in this process. Your goal is not to find published work that supports your point of view; rather, it is to find rigorous work that helps shape it.

As we define it, *topical research* refers to work (most often empirical) that has focused on the subject in which you are interested. While much of this work resides within academic journals and books, it may also be found in policy or government research, or in reports produced through foundations, not-for-profit and advocacy organizations. For example, suppose you are interested in studying factors that influence the decisions of homeless persons about whether or not to utilize shelters. Topical research in this area would profoundly shape how you might go about framing and conducting such a study. It offers insights on the nature and severity of the problem (the approximate size of the homeless population, the degree of underutilization or excess demand for shelters, and the consequences of underutilization), providing you with potential arguments for the study's significance. It also helps you identify gaps in the literature—what is not yet known about the topic. Finally, it allows you to survey the range of methodological approaches that have been brought to bear on the topic. This is a critical—and in our view overlooked—aspect of the literature review process. Reviewing the literature allows you not only to learn what is known about a topic, but to critically analyze how that topic has been investigated. Often, you learn that some approaches have yielded more robust research than others. In the study of homelessness described above, for instance, your review of the empirical research would show that the very process of quantifying the homeless population—determining the literal size of the issue—has long presented challenges for researchers, and that the methodology for doing so has evolved considerably since the topic was first explored (see Jencks, 1995).

In the terminology of Miles and Huberman (1994), it is topical research that helps us to fill the intellectual bins that make up our conceptual framework. (It also leads us to create new bins.) But as they also note, we too are interested in understanding the interrelationships among those bins. The purpose of a *theoretical framework* is just that.

The Oxford English Dictionary defines a framework as "a structure composed of parts framed together, *esp.* one designed for inclosing or supporting anything; a frame or skeleton." In the case of theoretical frameworks, the "parts" referred to in this definition are *theories*, and the thing that is being supported is the relationships embedded in the conceptual framework. More specifically, we argue that the parts are *formal* theories; those that emerge from and have been explored using empirical work. As such, the theories that comprise a theoretical framework are usually found in the scholarly literature. Theoretical frameworks may either be borrowed from other research (we will see an example of this in Chapter 3) or fashioned by the researcher for the purposes of the study at hand (as we describe in Chapter 3). In both cases, theoretical frameworks represent a combination or aggregation of formal theories in such a way as to illuminate some aspect of your conceptual framework.

Because theory can explain so many different types of relationships (a topic we address in detail in Chapter 2), theoretical frameworks are often multilayered and complex. What is critical is that they achieve cohesion across those layers. To return to the homelessness example from above, a theoretical framework may include theories that seek to explain why some homeless people refuse to use shelters, as well as theories that seek to explain how the categories that have traditionally framed this research (*the homeless* and *shelter*) ascribe value and desirability to certain behaviors (seeking shelter) while marginalizing others. In this case, the theoretical framework might call for a reconsideration of the meaning of these key categories, resulting in a different set of possible relationships between them. It might also raise questions about how the assumptions or position of the researcher (or of the field more generally) reinforces dominant or hegemonic views of the *subjects* (a term we view as problematic because it sets up hierarchy and is dehumanizing; we prefer the term *participants*) of the research, which in turn has implications for the study's methodology. (We will see an example of this use of theoretical frameworks in Chapter 4.) One way or another, the theoretical framework would articulate the relationship between how you think about homelessness and how you understand specific behaviors. This in turn would have significant implications for both the intellectual bins and interrelationships posited by the study's conceptual framework.

Another complicating factor in relating formal theories and theoretical frameworks to conceptual frameworks is that you should not do so uncritically. Just because a given theoretical framework "fits" a study does not mean that its validity or accuracy should be assumed. Developing a conceptual framework entails making arguments about how a given topic (and your approach to studying it) should be theorized, which means engaging theory critically. Further, as we see in the chapters to follow, at times what you learn in the field raises real challenges to the theories you used to design and carry out your research. Maxwell (2010) notes that this critical engagement with theory, especially when it is contradicted by what researchers learn in the field, remains all too rare in most research.

While we have attempted in this chapter to be as clear and specific as possible about what makes up a conceptual framework, it is important to caution the reader against oversimplification. By presenting topical research and theoretical frameworks as two different components of conceptual frameworks, we do not mean to imply that they are mutually exclusive. As we note, formal theory emerges from empirical work, and empirical research is frequently used to test or apply formal theory. Our purpose in differentiating these components is to note that they have different functions within a conceptual framework. Topical research describes the *what* of the study, while theoretical frameworks clarify the *why* and the *how*.

Additionally, while we have noted that conceptual frameworks allow you to make good decisions about how best to design and carry out an empirical study, we caution the reader not to view them as static. As Maxwell (in press) explains:

> Your conceptual framework will change during the course of your study, both because the information you gather will lead to new ideas and understandings, and because the process of doing this may lead you to become aware of, or question, parts of your previous conceptual framework.

As the following chapters make clear, a defining characteristic of conceptual frameworks is that they evolve. This may be in response to changes in the field, new insights from the literature, and/or findings from earlier rounds of data collection. Whatever the causes, it is highly unlikely that any study concludes with a conceptual framework identical to the one it started with. In most cases, the conceptual framework both informs and is informed by the conduct of research.

Lastly, while personal interests, empirical research, and theoretical frameworks comprise the major components of a conceptual framework, we would never expect to see one organized into these parts. In finished form, a conceptual framework is expressed as an argument. Each step of that argument is a proposition justified by the topical or theoretical literature. The chapters that follow present clear, robust examples of such arguments, each informed by personal interest and fusing together different empirical and theoretical work.

## ☆ DEFINING AND SITUATING CONCEPTUAL FRAMEWORKS: CONCLUDING THOUGHTS

The purpose of a conceptual framework is to learn from the experience and expertise of others as you cultivate your own knowledge and perspective. A conceptual framework allows you to make reasoned, defensible choices about how you might explore research topics or themes heretofore underexplored, explore existing research questions in new contexts, or reexamine established topics or questions using different theoretical or epistemological frames. Conceptual frameworks match your research questions with those choices, and in turn align your analytic tools and methods with your questions. Finally, conceptual frameworks offer a critical lens through which you may view your work and your role in carrying out that work.

The conceptual framework also guides the ways in which you think about collecting, analyzing, describing, and interpreting your data. It is a core, driving component of the empirical research cycle. It serves as a point of departure for you, and much later your audience, to define and explain other aspects of the study. The very development of guiding research questions, the literatures that are chosen for the literature review and how they are situated, and the sense of significance of the research as well as its relationship to broader discourse communities, are all grounded in your conceptual framework. This framework, as the title of our book suggests, helps you to conceptualize and articulate the reason, or rationale, for your research as well as supporting intellectual and methodological rigor; it helps determine the methodology and informs your research design in a recursive way.

# CHAPTER 2

# WHY CONCEPTUAL FRAMEWORKS?

In the previous chapter, we defined conceptual frameworks and situated our definition within the related literature. In this chapter, we make the case for their necessity. Conceptual frameworks, we argue, can help you resolve two common sources of ambiguity and confusion, evident both in the literature and, more important, in the common struggles and challenges faced by students embarking on major research projects. First, there is a lack of clarity and precision in understanding what the term *theory* means. Second, there is considerable confusion about the role and purpose of literature review as part of the empirical research process. If you are like most students, you hear your professors use these terms all the time, but you probably never hear them defined or explained in any detail. As a result, you learn that your research needs to include something called a literature review or a theoretical framework, but are less clear about how these pieces relate to one another or what their functions are. Organizing your thinking and work by developing and using a conceptual framework will simplify and clarify this process.

There has been no shortage of efforts to explore and explain the relationship between concepts, theories, frameworks, and methods (Anfara & Mertz, 2006). Some of these efforts seem to confuse rather than clarify these relationships. Others are clearly articulated and persuasively argued, but do not necessarily agree or fit with one another. Many of those who teach and mentor graduate students and novice researchers fail to adequately clarify their own understanding or working definitions of key terms or ideas relating to theory, conceptual frameworks, and the role of literature in empirical work, and thus use terms and concepts interchangeably. And even if you are lucky enough to have a professor or advisor who takes care to clearly define terms or concepts, the odds are that his is but one of several different (and potentially conflicting) voices you encounter as you prepare to carry out your own research. The field requires some realignment in this area. A primary goal of this book is to offer working concepts and definitions to address that need.

A thorough analysis of the extent and root causes of this confusion would require an empirical study of its own. The literature, after all, reflects the best efforts of people who purport to be thoroughly interested in this topic, and have presumably spent a great deal of time thinking about it. Focusing on the literature is therefore likely to *underestimate* the degree to which we as academics convey mixed, vague, or contradictory messages about how our students' research is shaped by the research of others. Even within this best-case scenario, however, it is not difficult to see where such messages might come from. We argue that there are two principle sources of confusion about how theory and literature inform research. First, the term *theory* refers to many things, but those who use the term with their students rarely explain what they mean by it (Maxwell, in press). Second, while the necessity of a literature review is widely agreed upon, there is considerable disagreement about why it is necessary (Boote & Beile, 2005; Maxwell, 2006). Further, we argue, the literature review tends to be viewed as a product rather than an iterative process of meaning and decision making that is guided by, as it informs, one's conceptual framework.

## ☆ WHAT (AND WHERE) IS THEORY?

Within the research lexicon, few terms are as frequently used and broadly defined as *theory*. Nearly everyone agrees that theory attempts to explain why things work the way that they do, and that it usually does so by way of identifying and examining relationships among things (Maxwell, 2005; Strauss, 1995). After that, it seems to get complicated and confusing for many.

Entire volumes have been dedicated to the question of what theory is. We cannot faithfully reproduce them here. To understand why this topic is confusing, however, we need only consider the multiple levels on which it is described. This is best accomplished by way of a scenario, as it (hopefully) avoids the overlapping and often vague terminology that characterizes many discussions of theory.

# THE MANY LEVELS OF THEORY: ☆
## A THOUGHT EXPERIMENT

Picture yourself in a room, looking at a page upon which you have drawn two boxes, the first labeled X, the second Y. There is a line connecting the two boxes. That line represents a relationship of some sort.

What you are looking at is a theory. That theory could be causal, as would be the case if X represented smoking and Y represented lung cancer. This is probably the most widely understood meaning of what theory is. But it could also be interpretive. Suppose, for example, that X represented race and Y denoted identity. It is unlikely that you would be suggesting that race *causes* identity. But you might very well be suggesting that it is an expression or function of it. In either case, you would be arguing that the *meaning* of race is somehow shaped by identity. Maybe, however, you are unsure of whether it is X or Y that is doing the shaping, or you hypothesize that the two are mutually influential. In this case, your theory would be primarily relational. Irrespective of the type of relationship between X and Y, all of these theories have two things in common. First, they are a logical assembly of conceptual pieces (Morse, 2004). Anfara and Mertz (2006) suggest that these pieces begin with sensations, which are then given names (concepts), which are then grouped (constructs), then related to one another (propositions), and finally ordered logically (theory). In our scenario, then, the diagram on the page might represent either a proposition or a theory, depending on what X and Y represent and the complexity of the relationship between them. Second, they are constrained to what is in the diagram. The concepts X and Y exist as independent constructs, treated as objects under study, and more or less accepted at face value. In the examples above, this means that it is assumed that we all have roughly the same ideas about what race and identity (or smoking and cancer) are, or at least what conceptual building blocks constitute them. This view of concepts and the relationships between them is often referred to as *postpositivism* (Creswell, 2005). This term has become something of a political hot potato in academia; those who wish to more fully engage this argument are invited to review the (many) publications arguing for or against it. For our purposes, we will simply note that the defining characteristic of this view of theory is that it concerns itself with concepts or constructs *as they are thought to exist*, and places less emphasis on questions of how or why they are thought to exist as such.

While likely the most obvious, the relationship between X and Y on the page in front of you is but one of many domains within which theory plays out in this scenario. A second domain takes into account the fact that it is *you* that has drawn the boxes and connecting line and *you* who is looking at the diagram. For this to occur, you must have accepted, at least conditionally, that there is such a thing as X, such a thing as Y, and some means by which they relate. The meaning of these things is, in this formulation, a function of your thinking about them; they hold no meaning outside of your interpretation of them. This is fairly easy to envision when X and Y denote abstractions such as race and identity, but it is worth pointing out that they are equally true of the first example given above, as both *smoking* and *cancer* allow ample room for interpretation that could substantively alter the hypothesized relationships between them. (The theorist Ivan Illich once corrected a journalist who had asked about his cancer by explaining that what he actually had was a cancer *diagnosis*.) While the first domain focused on the relationship between X and Y, this second domain focuses on the relationship between you and the diagram. It is concerned largely with issues of *epistemology*—how the individual constructs knowledge through the asking of questions. While undoubtedly theoretical in the sense of positing a relationship between thinker and thinking, this level of theory is often referred to in philosophical terms (Crotty, 1998; Guba, 1990). This is partly because it emerged as a critical response to positivism and objectivism, which held that the defining characteristic of scientific inquiry was that constructs such as X and Y could be observed objectively and atheoretically (Schwandt, 1993). But its implications extend beyond criticism. It encourages researchers to see themselves not merely as followers of scientific procedure but as interpreters and producers of it. It also explicitly defines research as an interpretive process: the way we collect and analyze data is a process of *making* rather than *discovering* meaning. This view of knowledge production forms the foundation for interpretivism and hermeneutics, two of the major paradigms informing social inquiry (Creswell, 2005; Denzin & Lincoln, 2003).

If you accept that the diagram is an extension of your thinking and not an objective image of "reality," the next question is: why do you think the way you do? What influences the processes through which you make meaning? How you conceptualize X and Y is not merely a function of your own eccentricities, after all. Your understanding of X and Y (and the relationship between them) is shaped by who you are, which is in turn shaped by the world around you. Who you are may be conceptualized in terms of age, race, gender, language, ethnicity, social class, or any number of other aspects of your being. It may be conceptualized in terms of an experience you have had. It is also fluid; how you see yourself, or which aspects of your self shape your understanding of something, likely depends on your context. A third domain of theory views the diagram as a cognitive or symbolic extension of yourself, and thus focuses on the relationship between the world outside the room and you. This is the primary focus of hermeneutics, which seeks to understand why interpretation happens as it does, and the types of linguistic and historical processes that influence the making of meaning (Gadamer, 1989; Ricoeur, 1973). It also gives rise to "critical" theories such as feminism, critical theory, critical race theory, queer theory, and aspects of Marxist theory, which posit that larger social structures and processes associated with race, gender, and social class profoundly shape how we come to understand social phenomena (Parker & Lynn, 2002; Skeggs, 2001).

Returning to the particulars of our scenario, a fourth domain of theory focuses on the room you are sitting in, and how its location (specific and broad) and characteristics may affect your production of the diagram. Suppose, for instance, that X referred to human activity and Y referred to global warming. One might easily imagine (or observe, in the ongoing political and cultural battles over climate change) that the definition of each, and the relationship between the two, would vary greatly in both nature and complexity depending on the institutional setting in which it is hypothesized. Specifically, we might postulate that certain institutional settings, themselves embedded in larger worlds, make certain understandings and ways of relating X and Y more or less available. Theorists such as Michel Foucault devoted their intellectual lives to exploring the ways in which the development and evolution of social institutions (for example, churches, hospitals, asylums, and prisons) fundamentally altered the conceptual categories (for example, virtue, health, sanity, and safety) available to individuals as they experienced and interpreted the world around them and thus circumscribed the choices they made (Mills, 2003). Philosophical traditions such as poststructuralism and postmodernism share a similar preoccupation with interrogating the production of "truth" and "rationality" and the social implications thereof (Lather, 2006). (In a mischievous bit of analysis, Becker [1993] points out that the terms under which arguments over the epistemology of social inquiry play out are themselves a product of the social organization of academic disciplines or fields.)

## WHOSE THEORY IS IT, AND WHERE DOES IT COME FROM? ☆

So far, we have focused primarily on what theory is about. To complicate matters further, there is the question of whose theory it is. Descriptions of theory range from informal hunches to formal sets of propositions that have guided, and been subject to, widespread empirical exploration (Lytle & Cochran-Smith, 1992; Noffke, 1999; Schön, 1995). Schwandt (2007) suggests that theory ranges from informally held *concepts* about why things work the way they do, to *theoretical orientations* used for "identifying, framing, and solving problems," to *substantive theories* focused on specific content rather than just relationships, to *formal theories*, which in essence are substantive theories that have achieved a level of generalizability (p. 292). Similarly, Marshall and Rossman (2006) differentiate between *tacit* and *formal* theories—the former referring to personally held ideas about how things work, the latter denoting established theory as found in the research literature. Maxwell (2005) adopts a similar view, noting that while *existing* theory frames and informs the research process, the assumptions and tentative hypotheses held by the researcher as she thinks through a study themselves constitute theory. Referring to an anecdote in which a student is interested in parent-infant interactions, Schram (2003) suggests that

> we can identify theory along a continuum that extends from formal explanatory axiom (Bowlby's Attachment Theory), to a tentative hunch ("Something about that interaction between mother and infant doesn't seem right"), to any general set of ideas that guide action ("It's more appropriate to ask the mother about it first"). (p. 42)

In other words, theory may posit a formal relationship, refer to a hunch held by the researcher/observer, or reflect a set of beliefs about how the topic itself should be studied.

There is nothing wrong with any of these levels, or characterizations, of theory. Each is useful; each says something important about how we go about figuring out how the world works and the factors that shape that process. The problem is that they are really quite different from one another, yet they all have the same name. The result was neatly summarized by Flinders and Mills (1993):

> When researchers speak of theory, they naturally take for granted that they will be understood at the level they intend to be understood. Yet, because these various levels of meaning are simultaneously at play, what researchers take for granted may not be shared by others. They sometimes find themselves talking about theory at one level, while their colleagues are thinking about it at quite another level. At best, this leads to muddled communication. At worst, researchers are left wondering how otherwise intelligent people could be so obtuse as to misunderstand what they mean. (p. xiv)

When a professor tells you that your work lacks a "theoretical framework," she could be referring to any of the domains of theory described above, or to some amalgam of domains. Is it any wonder that students are so often confused about where, when, and how theory informs their work?

Throughout *Reason and Rigor*, we aim to highlight how theory (at different levels) informs the conceptual frameworks of scholars from different fields, using different methods. While all of the researchers featured use theory to posit relationships between concepts, they vary considerably in the degree to which they explicitly theorize themselves (and the worlds they inhabit) into the research process. As we will see, this is due to a variety of factors, including the nature of the questions, the intended audience, and the field(s) in which the researcher works.

Assuming that you can somehow figure out what your professors mean by *theory*, how do you figure out how it informs your work? What theories (and what levels of theory) apply, given your interests? To answer these questions, you need to learn from the work of others. But here we run into a second, and equally serious, source of confusion: academics define and describe literature reviews in different ways, and do not necessarily agree on the purpose of reviewing literature.

## WHAT IS A LITERATURE REVIEW, AND WHAT IS IT FOR? ☆

As we began writing this book, we asked a dozen or so colleagues from across the country, all university-based scholars and researchers, to tell us how they view the role of the literature review in master's theses and dissertations as well as in scholarship more broadly. There was a wide range of responses, many of which contradicted each other. For some, it seems, developing a comprehensive literature review is about recreating our own graduate experiences (positive or not): we ask students to do it because we believe it to be a rite of passage for novice researchers, believing that it is arduous and time-consuming and that is what makes doctoral work rigorous. This view persists because those who have been put through this kind of process by their advisors are, in turn, more likely to subject their students to the same experiences. For others, the purpose of a literature review is to demonstrate expertise about a specific topic. This is partly out of the necessity of knowing one's subject, and partly from a sense of academic quid pro quo—if you want other people to care about what you think, you need to show that you care about what they think and that you know what a wide variety of scholars think. Still others view the literature review as a process of situating what one wants to study within a larger framework of information and ideas, in essence explaining how the empirical work at hand informs unresolved questions or gaps in the literature.

Several of our colleagues used a common metaphor to describe the literature review: a conversation. Yet their framing of this conversation differed in important ways. First, if a literature review is a conversation among scholars, is the student/author a participant in the conversation or an observer? Second, if the student is a participant, how much is he allowed to talk back? Is his role to sit at the table, ask questions, and nod solemnly, or is he free to engage with what he sees as problematic assumptions or ideas?

Our informal survey suggested there is no real consensus about what a literature review is for. Like the confusion about conceptual and theoretical frameworks, the role of the literature review in academic research is perplexing for many students, novice scholars, and researchers more broadly. The literature in this area, while considerable, does not necessarily ameliorate this confusion (Bruce, 1994; Boote & Beile, 2005). And even if academics could all agree on what a literature review is for, we often fail to adequately address those questions of greatest importance to students: how does the literature review relate to the design of the study more generally?

Literature reviews are generally defined in one of two ways. The first is as a subgenre of academic writing. A literature review in this sense is a comprehensive synthesis of all of the research literature about a specific topic. Typically, the author establishes criteria for which research to include, sometimes based on publication in peer-reviewed journals, other times based on data or methodology. The goal of this type of writing is to present to the reader a clear sense of the intellectual contours and fault lines within a given conceptual domain: What are the broad areas of agreement about a given topic, where are there disagreements, and why do they occur? What questions are unanswered? What overarching conclusions and lessons can be learned from the accumulated literature? This type of literature review includes several subgenres, including meta-analyses (in which analyses are aggregated to assess the overall strength of relationships or effect sizes across studies or data sets) and systemic reviews (where the overall strength of evidence for a specific intervention or treatment is assessed).

The second way of defining a literature review relates more specifically to theses and dissertations. The most common, and general, definition of the literature review in this sense is that it is a discussion of research literature related to one's topic (Bruce, 1994; Nunan, 1992). Hart (1998) defines a literature review as

the selection of available documents (both published and unpublished) on the topic, which contain information, ideas, data and evidence written from a particular standpoint to fulfill certain aims or express certain views on the nature of the topic and how it is to be investigated, and the effective evaluation of these documents in relation to the research being proposed. (p. 13)

Each of these definitions makes sense. The problem is that scholars do not tend to agree on whether they are two different things. One view suggests that mastery of one's field—a prerequisite for doctoral-level work—requires a comprehensive synthesis of all literature related to that field. This is necessary not only for the sake of learning relevant content and theory, but also for developing the skills of assimilating and synthesizing academic work (Hart, 1998; Boote & Beile, 2005). A second view suggests that the scope of the literature review should be confined to those works that are most relevant to the study's research questions. Maxwell (2006) discusses a "division within the educational research community as a whole over the proper form and goal of literature reviews that are part of dissertations and dissertation proposals" (p. 29). That division, he argues, is between the expectations of some faculty that a literature review must be thorough and comprehensive versus the view of others that it should be a selective and focused review of literature within and across specified fields. This inconsistency, he argues, is at the center of the confusion around the genre, its goals, and its uses. Maxwell offers a perspective on literature reviews that *relevance* is more important than *thoroughness*. He defines relevance in this way: "Relevant works are those that have important implications for the design, conduct, or interpretation of the study, not simply those that deal with the topic, or in the defined field of substantive area, of the research" (p. 28), and argues against what he refers to as Boote and Beile's "foundationalist" perspective on literature reviews, arguing instead to view them as an anchor or tool, stating that "a literature review is an essential tool, and any researcher must learn to use it competently" (p. 30).

There is also considerable variation in the literature regarding the purpose of literature reviews. While these differences are not so much a matter of disagreement as they are a product of different areas of focus, they still contribute to students' confusion. Overall, the literature suggests three major purposes for the literature review. First, it locates one's own work within the context of what is already known about a given topic or phenomenon. In this view, research is a collective, cumulative enterprise. The ultimate goal is the expansion of knowledge; it therefore stands to reason that new research should embark from the point up to which a topic or question is well defined or understood. Shulman (1999) asserts that *generativity*—or "building on one another's work" p. —is one of the primary criteria of solid scholarly work. He defines *generativity* as the way in which scholars make sophisticated and critical meaning of prior scholarship and research in order to situate our own work in a pre-existing milieu. Shulman states that "the key rationale for insisting on disciplined, public, and peer-reviewed work is to provide a sound basis for others to build atop one's efforts, even as each of us strives to stand on the shoulders of our peers. If the edifice of education scholarship is to achieve integrity, then the investigations that constitute that corpus of work must themselves have integrity" (p. 162). Boote and Beile (2005) echo this view, asserting that "a researcher cannot perform significant research without first understanding the literature in the field. . . . To be useful, and meaningful, education research must be cumulative; it must build on and learn from prior research and scholarship on the topic" (p. 3).

A second, and related, purpose of the literature review is to identify areas in which new scholarship is needed. In this approach, the literature review places scholarly texts in active conversation with preceding works with a primary goal of situating the current study to contribute to an existing corpus of scholarship through engagement, critique, and innovative reframing of text. In addition, the role of the literature review is not only to help shape the theoretical underpinnings of a study, but to help shape the methodological approach as well. As Glesne (2006) argues, reviewing the literature, and thus creating a knowledge of the literature, helps researchers to "judge whether your research plans go beyond existing findings and may thereby contribute to your field of study" (p. 24). Maxwell (2005, 2006) makes a similar point, arguing that the literature review must situate a body of literature in broader scholarly and historical contexts and examine claims and their methodological justification, thereby helping the author understand what still needs to be investigated in the field. The literature review must summarize and synthesize existing literature in ways that allow for new perspectives to emerge.

A third purpose of the literature review, and one that we find is often overlooked, is to inform research design and methodology. Hart, whose widely used book *Doing a Literature Review: Releasing the Social Science Research Imagination* (1998) makes the argument that a dissertation literature review must clearly integrate and synthesize prior research to create new understandings, articulate what next questions a study must ask and why a proposed study is important to the field, and make an argument for its own methods as well. He further notes that

> a major benefit of the review is that it ensures the "researchability" of your topic before "proper" research commences. All too often students new to research equate the breadth of their research with its value. Initial enthusiasm, combined with this common misconception, often results in broad, generalized and ambitious proposals. It is the progressive *narrowing* of the topic, through the literature review, that makes most research a practical consideration. (p. 13)

In this sense, the literature review helps one to focus one's topic and the scope of one's research substantively, not just to contextualize the topic and research questions.

In a similar vein, Boote and Beile (2005) argue that a thorough literature review is essential to developing the theoretical and methodological sophistication needed to make good decisions about research design and methods. They argue that this use of literature is all too often overlooked.

> Current initiatives and faculty focuses have ignored the centrality of the literature review in research preparation, in turn weakening the quality of education research. This oversight has its roots, we believe, in a too-narrow conception of the literature review—as merely an exhaustive summary of prior research—and a misunderstanding of its role in research. . . . A good literature review is the basis of both theoretical and methodological sophistication, thereby improving the quality and usefulness of subsequent research. (pp. 3–4)

These three purposes are not contradictory. In fact, they might best be viewed hierarchically. Taken together, they suggest that in order to thoroughly review the literature, the researcher must (1) understand the conversation already happening; (2) figure out how to add to this conversation; and (3) identify the best means of doing so theoretically and methodologically. A handful of scholars have advanced precisely this view (Glesne, 2006; Hart, 1998). Why, then, is there such confusion among students about the nature and purpose of literature review?

For one thing, our experience suggests that students hear quite a bit about the first and second purposes but much less about the third. The guidance you receive about literature reviews tends to focus heavily on finding out what is known about a given topic, and much less about how (and how well) it came to be known. As Boote and Beile (2005) note, many published guides to conducting literature reviews underscore this bias. The result is research design and methodology that are divorced from the literature. This not only makes many literature reviews incoherent (Locke, Spirduso, & Silverman, 2007), it dramatically dilutes their value for the research itself.

A second contributing factor is the tendency to think of the literature review as more of a product than a process. Too much emphasis is placed on the literature review as a component of dissertations or published research— a task to be completed and checked off—rather than as an active process of sense making that helps the researcher synthesize and integrate within and across various existing theories and bodies of scholarship. Above all, the purpose of literature review is *learning*. It is the process through which you become informed about what is known about a given topic, what is not known, and how others have attempted to answer relevant questions related to that topic. Viewed this way, the thoroughness-relevance relationship shifts from one that appears dichotomous to one that is developmental. The purpose of reviewing literature is to arrive at an understanding of what is most relevant, both to the field and to the research design. The road to relevance passes through thoroughness. The remaining question—how much of the literature review to include in the final product—strikes us as less important and interesting than what is learned along the way and how it informs the work.

A third, and related, problem lies in the artificial separation of the literature review from other structural elements of the dissertation, including the conceptual/theoretical framework and methodology. Reviewing dissertation drafts, it is not uncommon for us to find separate sections titled "Statement of the Problem," "Conceptual Framework," "Theoretical Framework," and "Methodology" in addition to a chapter titled "Literature Review." Yet each of these sections actually reviews the literature!

Particularly perplexing is the common practice of separating one's "statement of the problem" or "purpose of the study" from the wider literature review. One commonly used guide to writing dissertation proposals, for example, defines the problem statement as an introduction to the study that describes "the big issue you want to address" (Biklen & Casella, 2007, p. 56), while the literature review (presented as a thing rather than a process) is a summary of "the conversation that already exists in relation to your topic" (p. 76).

This strikes us as problematic for two reasons. First, as we note above, arguing for the importance of your study should be the product of reviewing the literature, not a parallel activity. Second, suggesting that this one small section of your study is the designated place for argument implies that the rest of your study is not such a place. By now it should be apparent that we view the whole of your study as an argument, and much of it an outgrowth of the process of reviewing literature.

## ☆ THE CASE FOR CONCEPTUAL FRAMEWORKS: CONCLUDING THOUGHTS

This chapter has focused on the reasons why students and new researchers tend to get lost inside all of the different elements of the research process. In sum, we argue that students tend to be confused not by a lack of ideas about what theory is or what literature review is for, but by a profusion of such ideas with no clear mechanism or framework for sorting them out or relating them to one another. This confusion is compounded by disagreement about how both theory and literature are intended to inform and structure research. Some scholars (Anfara & Mertz, 2006; Dressman, 2008) evoke an "off the shelf" view of theory, as in *I am using social reproduction theory to study the educational experience of second-generation Central American immigrants.*

Others caution students to resist precisely this approach, suggesting that premature adoption or overreliance on theory forces the researcher to narrow his focus, blinding him to possible avenues of inquiry in his work (Anderson & Jones, 2000; Avis, 2003; Van Maanen, 1988). As noted above, disagreements also abound with regard to literature reviews, principally with regard to their scope, but also in the degree to which the literature is intended to inform research design and methodology.

This overall confusion and lack of coherence will not be resolved by renaming things (or worse yet, arguing about which things should get which names). What will help, however, is if researchers can learn to be as clear and explicit as possible about why and how we have chosen to study a topic, and can learn to use the process of literature review to develop, refine, and evolve these arguments. This book is intended to promote this type of transparency and coherence. In the chapters that follow, we highlight and analyze the work of four exceptional scholars, each of whom has demonstrated how to frame and argue for his or her work as well as how to let those arguments inform, and be informed by, his or her empirical work.

# CHAPTER 3

# EXCAVATING QUESTIONS

## *Conceptual Frameworks and Research Design*

While it is undoubtedly true that research questions shape research design, such questions do not simply materialize out of the academic ether. To paraphrase Winston Churchill, arriving at your research questions is not so much the beginning as the end of the beginning. But you have to engage in significant intellectual work to get there. The conceptual framework, we argue, serves as both guide and ballast throughout the process of refining one's understanding of the domain of inquiry as well as the questions that will guide the inquiry into fruition.

## "EXCAVATING" RESEARCH QUESTIONS ☆

The process of developing your research questions is primarily one of *excavation*. You disembark onto a vast swath of intellectual terrain, formed by an amalgam of what you care about and are interested in, the field(s) you have been exposed to and are working within, and what is already known about the problems or questions that pique your interest. Somewhere buried within that mass of interests, concerns, and exposures are your research questions. To find these questions, you must dig deeply into significant amounts of written material: texts that fit specifically into your domain of study, as well as those not directly related to your research questions but that may help contextualize them. This process begins with the development of broad, topical distinctions that help you figure out what is and is not relevant to the central topics of your emerging study. From this entry point, you move to questions of what is already known and established in the fields that relate to your topic. This process of wading through—and making meaning of—the fields that relate to and frame your emerging research helps you determine what is already known about these fields and what is not yet known. It is here that you begin to build your conceptual framework. What is already known, and *how* it is known, form the foundation upon which your research questions, and ultimately your research design, will be built. From there it is a process of searching, with increasing sensitivity and sophistication, for ideas, theories, and methods that help you to figure out what is most important for you to ask, how best to ask it, and how to structure an empirical study so that you are in a position to answer your research questions in data-based ways.

In this chapter, we illustrate the interconnection between conceptual frameworks and research design, focusing on James P. Spillane's (2002) "Local Theories of Teacher Change: The Pedagogy of District Policies and Programs." After providing intellectual background and context for the article and presenting excerpts from the published work itself, we offer a detailed analysis of the argument that constitutes its conceptual framework. We then explain how choices made about the conceptual framework in turn shape the research design, directly influencing data collection and analysis in myriad ways. We conclude with a discussion of the interrelated and evolving nature of conceptual frameworks and their relationship to research design.

## ☆ ABOUT THE AUTHOR

In the field of education policy research, few contemporary scholars have been as innovative or as influential as James Spillane. Collaborating with colleagues in Michigan, he was part of a group of scholars that pioneered a new view of policy implementation focused on how actors at various levels of the educational system make sense of policy, and how their understanding of policy in turn shaped how they implemented it. Spillane's specific contributions to this work include analyses of the social and interactive nature of teachers' thinking and learning about policy (Spillane, 1999), explorations of how local officials construct policy through interpretation of various "signals" from the state and elsewhere (Spillane, 2000, 2004), and local officials' theories about how teachers learn (Spillane, 2002, presented below). Spillane has also pioneered a *distributed perspective* on school leadership, a view that has fundamentally changed the way that researchers (and many practitioners) in education and beyond think about leadership work in schools.

In addition to his many conceptual and theoretical contributions to the field of educational policy, Spillane has also been a key innovator in research methods. His studies have employed a vast array of data collection and analysis strategies, including traditional participant observation and survey research, real-time electronic logs of principal activity, and quantitative social network analyses as a strategy for measuring school communication and interpersonal influence. He has published extensively on his innovations in mixed methods research.

James P. Spillane is the Spencer T. and Ann W. Olin Professor in Learning and Organizational Change at the School of Education and Social Policy at Northwestern University, where he is a faculty associate at the Institute for Policy Research and director of the Multidisciplinary Doctoral Program in Education Science. His publications can be found in *American Educational Research Journal, Cognition and Instruction, Educational Evaluation and Policy Analysis, Education Researcher, Journal of Curriculum Studies, Teacher's College Record, Educational Policy, Journal of Educational Policy,* and *Journal of Research on Science Teaching.* He has served as associate editor of *Educational Evaluation and Policy Analysis* and serves on the editorial board of many journals, including *Journal of Research on Science Teaching, Elementary School Journal,* and *Cognition and Instruction.* He is author of *Standards Deviation: How Schools Misunderstand Policy* (2004) and *Distributed Leadership* (2006), and coeditor of *Distributed Leadership in Practice* with John Diamond of Harvard University (2007). He received a Fulbright Distinguished American Scholars Award from the New Zealand Fulbright Committee in 2002.

## BACKGROUND AND CONTEXT: AN ☆ OVERVIEW OF THE WORK IN FOCUS

At the heart of all policy implementation is the complex process of changing human behavior. Social policies are in essence plans that are designed to get people—whether teachers, doctors, consumers, or voters—to behave in ways that are thought to benefit them or the people they are supposed to serve. Policy implementation is the process of putting those plans into action. For a long time, the dominant framework for thinking about implementation was built upon concepts from economics and political science: rewards or sanctions introduced in such a way as to inform rational choice.

But what if the people who are supposed to implement policy see it as something wholly different than do those who designed it? Incentives or disincentives for implementing a policy may serve us well if everyone shares the same fundamental understanding of what the policy actually is, but what if they don't? What if they think it means different things? What if policy implementation is less like reading from a script and more like interpreting an image? If this were the case, the fundamental challenge of implementation would be less about incentives and more about understanding.

The article we discuss in this chapter seeks to better understand policy implementation as a process of teaching and learning. We analyze "Local Theories of Teacher Change: The Pedagogy of District Policies and Programs" (Spillane, 2002), in which the author explores the relationship between district actors' theories of teacher learning and classroom practice. This article originally appeared in *Teachers College Record* and is an outgrowth of Spillane's wider study of the Statewide Systemic Initiative (SSI), an early state-level reform focused on standards-based reform in mathematics and science. This wider study has been described in detail in numerous articles (see Spillane, 1996, 1998, 1999, 2000) and in Spillane's 2004 book, *Standards Deviation: How Schools Misunderstand Education Policy.* The article presented here found its origins in a series of analyses conducted toward the end of the SSI study. While the article presented below has its own specific conceptual framework, it emerges from and builds on the framework of the wider study. The SSI study framed policy interpretation as a critical aspect of implementation. In other words, how educators understood a given policy was directly related to the actions they took in implementing it. In *Standards Deviation*, Spillane specifically engaged in a critique of research that views implementation as a matter of fidelity (that is, policies are consciously followed or rejected) or that employs a rational choice model in which local players deliberately choose to accept, reject, or modify policy. As Spillane asserts:

> Conventional accounts assume that local officials are choosing between following policymakers' directions or ignoring them; they assume that locals get the intended policy message. That assumption is problematic because in order to choose, local actors must figure out what the policy means. To decide whether to ignore, alter, or adopt policymakers' recommendations, local officials must construct an understanding of the policy message. (Spillane, 2004, p. 6)

Further, Spillane argues that the ways in which policy is understood is a complex and situated process. Effectively, he makes the case that district actors do not merely implement policy, they make it. Their process of doing so, he asserts, is based on the incorporation and interpretation of information from a variety of sources, including official state policy. This way of thinking about implementation was, at the time of the research, relatively unusual. The conventional view still focused on "rational choice" and with it the assumption that the policy message was understood as intended. But Spillane was part of a group of scholars in Michigan in the early 1990s that were beginning to think in new and innovative ways about this process. In studying the adoption of mathematics frameworks in California, David Cohen, Deborah Ball, Susanna Wilson, Penelope Peterson, and others were coming to think of policy implementation by teachers not as a matter of following (or resisting), but rather as a form of learning (see Cohen & Ball, 1990). From this perspective, implementation was not a matter of fidelity, but rather the process through which teacher (or principal) learning occurred. This idea influenced both Spillane's formulation of the SSI study and the conceptual framework for "Local Theories of Teacher Change."

Methodologically, Spillane's focus on interpretation necessitated a qualitative approach, as he needed data that would allow him to examine and understand how actors at various levels of the system understood and interpreted policy. But he had a challenge: asking specifically about state policy would likely constrain the interviews, generating the very types of normative responses that Spillane was arguing against. So for the interview component, he adopted a more open, less structured and directive format. For districts, for example, he used snowball sampling—developing a participant pool based on key respondents' suggestions of who else would provide valuable perspectives—to try to find the people in each district who were most knowledgeable about math and science instruction. In the interviews themselves, open-ended, semistructured protocols focused largely on how district officials thought about and supported standards and instruction. The goal was to create the conditions necessary to engage respondents in talking openly about math and science instruction on, and in, their own terms.

At the same time, the SSI study was in part an evaluation of how the new state standards affected practice. Studying instruction in an evaluative context is challenging work. Documenting change in instruction calls for both sufficient detail and depth of understanding to be sensitive to those changes and sufficient scale to measure their breadth and significance. Few studies have the resources to do so fully, so trade-offs have to be made. In this case, the trade-off was to use surveys to get a general sense of teachers' instructional practice, but then to engage in close observations on a subsample to try to obtain a more fine-grained view of how instruction was being shaped. This need to explore, in an inductive way, how players in the setting engage in and think about these issues is, in large part, how the study ended up including interview data on districts and teachers, as well as survey and observation data at the teacher level.

As indicated in the excerpt that follows, "Local Theories of Teacher Change" both builds on and extends the conceptual framework that guided the SSI study. It uses the findings from the wider study to develop and contextualize a new set of research questions, and while it relies on the same data set as the original study, it employs new analytic approaches in accordance with modifications in the conceptual framework. In the remainder of this chapter, we first present an excerpt from the published article. We next highlight the article's conceptual framework, noting how it builds on the argument of the wider study. We then illustrate how the refined framework led to a new set of analytic approaches, and we draw broader connections between the conceptual framework and research design. This analysis highlights the relationship between the conceptual framework and research methods as well as the evolving and dynamic nature of the framework itself.

> Spillane, J. P. (2002). Local theories of teacher change: The pedagogy of district policies and programs. *Teachers College Record*, *104*, 377–420; *Teachers College Record* by Columbia University. Copyright 2002 Reproduced with permission of Teachers College Record in the format Textbook via Copyright Clearance Center.

## Situating the Work: Theoretical Underpinnings

[1] A combination of pressure including bureaucratic control and accountability mechanisms, and support in the form of curricular materials and professional development, is thought necessary if teachers are to implement instructional reform proposals (Elmore & McLaughlin, 1988; McDonnell & Elmore, 1987). In the segmented and decentralized American education system, many governmental and nongovernmental agencies provide support and sometimes apply pressure to guide teachers' practice. Pressure, though necessary, is believed to be insufficient for local implementation (Elmore & McLaughlin, 1988). Support is essential, and the local work setting, because of its proximity to the classroom, is possibly the most influential environment with respect to teacher support.

[2] Support is especially important with respect to the implementation of standards-based reform because the complex changes in instruction that characterize these reform proposals will require

substantial learning by those who are expected to implement these changes (Cohen & Barnes, 1993). Teachers, often unwittingly, understand instructional reform proposals to involve only minor changes in their existing conceptions of teaching, learning, and subject matter (EEPA, 1990; Spillanc & Zeuli, 1999). Even if teachers construct the reform message in ways that resonate with its intent, they may lack the requisite knowledge to put it into practice. Hence, teachers will have to learn a great deal to successfully implement the tremendous changes in instruction pressed by standards-based reforms (Cohen & Barnes, 1993; Schifter, 1996). This learning is difficult, both for the teachers and for those who teach them, because the new disciplinary content and pedagogy represent such a tremendous shift from how teachers now teach and how they learned in school. Further, this learning depends in some measure on the capability of district officials, both administrators and lead teachers, to promote teacher learning from and about standards. District officials' support of teachers' learning from and about standards will depend not only on their understanding of the instructional ideas advanced through these reforms but also on their ideas about communicating these understandings to teachers; that is, their beliefs about and knowledge of teacher learning. One's understanding of a policy message does not ensure that one can help others understand that message.

[3]  To say that teachers will have to learn so they can to implement the instructional reforms advanced through standards, however, leaves much unspecified and underexplored because learning can be conceptualized in different ways. Learning in general, and teacher learning in particular, can mean different things depending on one's conceptual perspective (Richardson, 1999). Thus, in suggesting that implementation involves learning, it is necessary to probe the nature of learning. To do that, I look at theories of learning using a typology developed by Greeno, Collins, and Resnick (1996). They identify three theoretical perspectives on cognition and learning—behaviorism, the cognitive view, and the situative-sociohistoric view.

[4]  The behaviorist perspective, associated with B. F. Skinner, holds that the mind at work cannot be observed, tested, or understood; thus, behaviorists are concerned with actions (behavior) as the sites of knowing, teaching, and learning. Knowledge is transmitted by teachers and received, but not interpreted, by students. Transmission is the instructional mode, and to promote effective and efficient transmission, complex tasks are decomposed into

hierarchies of component subskills that must be mastered in sequence from simple to complex (Gagne, 1965). Learning is externally motivated by reward and requires developing correct reactions to external stimuli. Well-organized routines of activity, clear instructional goals with frequent feedback and reinforcement, and the sequencing of skills from simpler to more complex are important in the design of learning opportunities.

[5] The situative-sociohistoric perspective (Hutchins, 1995a, 1995b; Lave, 1988; Pea, 1993; Resnick, 1991; Vygotsky, 1978) regards individuals as inseparable from their communities and environments. This perspective views knowledge as distributed in the social, material, and cultural artifacts of the environment. Knowing is the ability of individuals to participate in the practices of communities (e.g., the mathematics community). Learning involves developing practices and abilities valued in specific communities and situations. The motivation to engage in learning is seen in terms of developing and sustaining learners' identities in the communities in which they participate. Thus, learning opportunities need to be organized so that they encourage participation in practices of inquiry and learning, support the learner's identity as skilled inquirer, and enable the learner to develop the disciplinary practices of discourse and argumentation. Learning opportunities need to be grounded in problems that are meaningful to the student.

[6] The cognitive perspective (Piaget, 1970) seeks to understand and describe the working of the mind. Knowledge, in this view, includes reflection (Brown, 1978), conceptual growth and understanding, problem solving (Newell & Simon, 1972), and reasoning. Learning involves the active reconstruction of the learner's existing knowledge structures, rather than passive assimilation or rote memorization, with learners using personal resources including their prior knowledge and experiences to construct new knowledge (Anderson & Smith, 1987; Confrey, 1990). In this view, engagement with learning is natural. The motivation to learn is intrinsic. Moreover, extrinsic motivators can undermine intrinsic motivation (Lepper & Greene, 1979). Learning activities engage students' interest and prior knowledge, sequence their conceptual development, and introduce students to the core principles of a domain. This view of learning resembles what Richardson terms the normative-re-education perspective on teacher learning, in which change is enabled through reflection on one's beliefs and knowledge.

## Data Collection

[7] State-level data, collected between 1989 and 1996, included interviews with state policy makers, state legislation, Department of
Education (MDE) and State Board policy documents, State Board
meeting minutes, and media reports. District data included interviews with district officials and local policy documents, including
curriculum guides, annual reports, policy statements, and listings
of professional development workshops. A snowballing technique
was used to identify local educators involved in the instructional
policy making process for interviews. Those interviewed in each
district included district office and school administrators, teachers
involved in developing instructional policies, local school board
members, and parents. We completed 165 interviews.

[8] Interview protocols were used to ensure that comparable data
were collected across the 9 sites. These protocols included questions about general characteristics of the school district, the extent
and nature of district office efforts to reform mathematics and science, the ideas about mathematics and science instruction supported by district office reform initiatives, and the role of state and
federal policies in district office reforms. Interview questions were
open ended and interviews ranged from 45 minutes to 2 hours; all
but two were tape-recorded and transcribed. Based on an analysis
of first round interviews (collected in the autumn of 1994), a second round of data collection was undertaken the following spring.
District officials were asked a series of questions to get at their
beliefs about instructional change and teacher learning as part of a
broader conversation about standards and efforts to implement
standards in their district.

[9] The classroom component of the study used the Population 1
(third and fourth grade) and Population 2 (seventh and eighth
grade) Teacher Questionnaire of the Third International
Mathematics and Science Study (TIMSS) to survey all third- and
fourth-grade teachers and all seventh- and eighth-grade mathematics and science teachers in the 9 districts. Identifying a set of items
related to the mathematics standards, we constructed a scale of
reformed practice, and based on teachers' responses to these
items, we observed and interviewed a subsample of teachers, who
reported instruction that was more aligned with the mathematics
and science standards. Stratifying the sample to ensure distribution

across district types, locations within the state, and teachers who scored high on our reform scale, we then selected randomly from among the teachers reporting instruction that was aligned with the standards, approximately the top 10% of our sample. Focusing on teachers who reported teaching in ways that resonated with the standards enabled us to understand the nature of practice in classrooms where it was more likely to be consistent with standards and the implementation challenges faced by teachers.

[10] The subsample selected for observation and interviews included 32 teachers from 6 of the 9 districts. Of these 32 teachers, there were 18 third- or fourth-grade mathematics teachers, and seven were seventh- and eighth-grade mathematics teachers. We observed and interviewed each teacher twice, with the exception of one elementary teacher who was observed only once because of scheduling difficulties. During visits to these classrooms, we used an observation protocol to take detailed notes about practice and audiotaped parts of lessons. After each observation, we wrote field notes of our observations, including a detailed narrative of the lesson we observed that addressed each of the analytical issues identified in the protocol. We also interviewed the teacher following each observation, audiotaping each interview.

## Data Analysis

[11] All interview data were computer coded. Five categories were used to code first-round interviews: background information on the site; ideas about mathematics and science supported by district office policies; consistency, authority, power and authority of local policies; teachers' opportunities to learn about instruction in the district; and local perspectives on state and federal policies. Second-round interviews were coded for local educators' understandings of mathematics and science for "all students," mathematical "problem solving," "hands-on" science, and parental involvement.

[12] For the purpose of this paper, we reanalyzed interview data with those district officials in the sample who took a central role in selecting or designing learning opportunities for teachers. Initially, we identified all passages that focused on instructional change and teacher learning from the interview transcripts of those 44 district and school administrators, lead teachers, and subject-matter specialists who were involved on a regular basis in promoting instructional

change in their district. We not only looked at district officials' responses to those questions that focused explicitly on their beliefs about teacher learning and instructional change but also looked at their entire transcripts for relevant data. We then coded the data for each informant, using four categories that focused on their beliefs about teaching teachers, teacher learning, the curriculum for teacher learning, and motivating teachers to learn and change. Four of the 44 informants were removed from the sample because there was insufficient data with respect to their beliefs about teacher learning. Two researchers then coded data for the remaining informants using three categories—behaviorist, cognitive, and situated—to categorize each informant's theories about instructional change and teacher learning. Inter-rater reliability was 75%, with the two coders agreeing initially on the categorization of 30 of the 40 informants. After discussing the data for the remaining informants, the two coders agreed on the categorization of nine of them, engaging a third researcher to classify the remaining informant.

\* \* \*

[13] Phase 3 qualitative data were analyzed and integrated with the TIMMS questionnaire data to examine what aspects of instruction were consistent with the standards and what forces were influencing teachers' implementation. Classroom observation and interview data were coded using categories that corresponded to the content and pedagogy standards put forward by NCTM [National Council of Teachers of Mathematics], along with the category "all students" (concerning issues of race, class, gender, and handicapping conditions). The coding of data involved interpreting and organizing narrative accounts of the lessons and teachers' interview responses in light of the coding categories. These analyses resulted in analytical memos that ranged from 40 to 90 single-spaced pages for each teacher. Further, these data were coded for the array of factors that interact to influence teachers' attempts to revise their practice including policy, professional, private, and public sectors as well as influences associated with teachers' personal experiences and their students.

## THE ARGUMENT ☆

As we define it, a conceptual framework is a grounded argument about why the topic of a study matters to its various and often intersecting fields, why the methodological approach used to explore that topic is valid, and the ways in which the research design is appropriate and the methods are rigorous. In "Local Theories of Teacher Change," that argument is presented as follows:

1. Reform implementation is a function of pressure and support. Support is most effectively provided at the local level (paragraph 1).

2. Standards-based reforms, which focus on instructional change, require substantial learning on the part of teachers (paragraph 2).

3. Local support therefore requires that districts be effective in promoting teacher learning (paragraph 2).

4. Learning is not a simple process, however. How districts support and promote teacher learning depends greatly on how learning is conceptualized (paragraph 3).

5. The research literature suggests three theoretical perspectives on learning: the behaviorist, cognitive, and situative-sociohistoric views (paragraph 3).

6. Data collected for this study allow for the analysis of both how district actors conceptualize teacher learning and the instructional practices of a subsample of teachers (paragraphs 7–10).

7. Data analysis focused on (a) the extent to which the theories of learning of local officials could be classified as behaviorist, cognitive, or situative-sociohistoric; and (b) the relationship between these theories of learning and the prevalence of instructional practices consistent with reform expectations (paragraphs 11–15).

Several aspects of this argument warrant further consideration. First, there is the question of what is assumed: what does the reader need to have in mind for Step 1 to make sense or to seem important? In this case, what is assumed is that implementation matters. It is assumed that the reader knows that the success of reforms hinges on their implementation, and that this is no small feat. There is a wealth of research literature supporting this point, but the author elects not to dwell on it, choosing instead to begin with a concise summary of what makes implementation work (pressure and support).

Any argument begins with this formulation: what does your audience already know and care about? In this case, Spillane assumes that his audience (readers of *Teachers College Record* in particular and education scholars more generally) cares about school reform and knows that implementation matters and that it is complicated. Were he presenting this paper at a conference of school counselors or parents, he might have to back up further to make his case. The audience might not be familiar with school reform at all, and it might hold different assumptions about the relationship between theory (reform on paper) and execution (reform in practice).

It is also helpful to examine what comprises the conceptual framework here. Specifically, it includes three parts: (1) previous empirical work on school reform implementation; (2) previous research conducted by the author about the nature and process of implementation; and (3) theoretical work on how learning happens. Previous research is introduced to support the idea of implementation as guided by pressure and support, and that classroom-level implementation is a function of teacher learning. In the case of the former, a widely read and cited source (Elmore & McLaughlin, 1988) is used to substantiate this rather broad claim. In the case of the latter, Spillane cites his own previous work along with that of his colleagues, David Cohen and Carol Barnes, who were studying implementation of mathematics reform in California around the same time the SSI study was conducted. This is an excellent example of how a discussion of literature moves from the general to the specific, and from widely read and accepted work to more nuanced and local research. In two paragraphs, Spillane brings the reader from some of the most generalized observations about reform into a particular conceptualization of what implementation looks like.

More subtly, Spillane also brings the reader up to date with the evolution of his own thinking about implementation. Like his colleagues in Michigan, Spillane had previously explored classroom-level implementation as a form of learning, and ventured theories about the contexts and processes through which that learning occurred (Spillane, 1999). He had also delved into the ways in which district officials learned state policy, and theorized about its effects on implementation (Spillane, 2000). At the time of "Local Theories of Teacher Change," however, he had not analyzed how actors at one level of the system thought about how those at other levels of the system learn policy. Such thinking, he reasoned, was likely embedded in local officials' ideas about school-level implementation, but up to 2002 this had not been a focus of his research.

The jump from viewing policy implementation as learning to viewing it as teaching—the flip side of the education coin—had been made previously by Cohen and Barnes (1993). If all policy required education of some sort, they asked:

> What kind of education has educational policy offered to enactors? What has been the pedagogy of policy? To answer these questions, we must inquire about how policymakers actually tried to teach teachers to teach differently, and to do that we must consider policy as a sort of instruction. (pp. 209–210)

Implicit (and occasionally explicit) in any conversation about how to teach are assumptions about how people learn. It is this facet of policy "education" that Spillane chose to focus on in "Local Theories of Teacher Change." The conceptual framework presented in the article can therefore be viewed as an extension of both Spillane's previous work and of Cohen and Barnes's analysis of the "pedagogy" of policy.

One useful way to think about developing a conceptual framework is that as the author, you are leading your readers down a path. At the end of the path is what you want to show them—your empirical study, as defined and framed by your research questions. But you need to get them there first. Each step on the path is a step in the argument. To this point in "Local Theories" (through paragraph 3 above), Spillane has walked his readers halfway down the path. He has made a strong case that successful policy implementation depends on how local officials think about teacher learning. In this sense, he has already satisfied one of the two main requirements of a good conceptual framework: he has made a strong argument that his topic matters and, further, has provided a rationale for how it matters. What he has not done (yet) is made the case for how he wants to explore this topic.

## ☆ CONCEPTUAL FRAMEWORKS AND RESEARCH DESIGN

When researchers get into questions of how a study is conducted, there is sometimes a tendency to assume that we have moved from a discussion of topic to a discussion of methods. In reality, it is not that simple. How you execute a study is a function of how you think about it. Both your research questions and your methods are shaped by your engagement with the literature. In the article presented here, the first step Spillane takes in convincing the reader that his approach is the right one is a theoretical one. As he rightly notes, merely saying that conceptions of learning are central to implementation is not enough:

> Teacher learning . . . can mean different things depending on one's conceptual perspective (Richardson, 1999). Thus, in suggesting that implementation involves learning, it is necessary to probe the nature of learning. (Spillane, 2002, p. 379)

This leaves Spillane facing a critical question: how do you "probe the nature of learning"? Recall that the primary analytic approach to the wider SSI study was inductive. Spillane explored and examined how local officials and teachers constructed policy in the context of their own practice. One option would have been to continue in that vein, analyzing the interview data with an eye toward developing a typology of local theories of learning. This would have been entirely defensible, provided there were sufficient data to define and support such a typology. But Spillane was not sure it was necessary. "You often reach a point where this is a toss-up," he explained in our interview about "Local Theories of Teacher Change" and his work more broadly. He continued:

> Do we need grounded theory here? There's a lot written about learning and change. There's a lot of work on learning theory. There's a lot written about teacher learning. So I guess I felt that it was unclear to me that there was a need to keep on the grounded theory and let the ideas bubble up at me.

The alternative to working inductively (letting the ideas "bubble up") was to analyze the data deductively by applying a previously developed, or a priori, set of themes or categories to them. Such themes are almost always derived from the research literature; in Spillane's case the vast, multidisciplinary literature on learning theory. Specifically, Spillane adopted a typology developed by Greeno, Collins, and Resnick (1996), which is itself a synthesis of the literature on how learning happens. In our working definition of a conceptual framework, this is an excellent example of how a *theoretical framework* (the Greeno et al. typology) becomes situated within a larger conceptual framework (the overall argument for the focus and execution of the study). As described in paragraphs 4 through 6, this typology presents three clearly defined and differentiated perspectives on learning, situating each within a rich empirical tradition. It therefore provides Spillane with a useful tool for "probing the nature of learning," one that informs both his thinking and his methodology.

There are two reasons for moving from an inductive to a deductive analytic approach. First, as the sociologist Andrew Abbot (2004) has said, research is a process of framing, reframing, and trying to solve puzzles. Our own intellect is one tool for solving those puzzles, but so are other people's intellects. A critical component of empirical research, and a major reason for consulting the literature to begin with, is using other people's ideas to help address our questions. As Spillane stated in our interview, "It helps you interpret the data, which is, after all, why we have conceptual frameworks." He continued:

> Here what you see is a shift to letting the ideas dominate—and these are ideas about learning—come to the fore and guide the conversation with the evidence, in many respects. But that is after reading through this data over and over again and trying to make some sense of it, and then

deciding this is not a situation where it is going to bubble up from below, and I need some conceptual and analytical tools to inform them.

The second reason for moving from an inductive to a deductive analytical approach is that the typologies developed through local, inductive work are rich in detail and nuance, but because they are emergent they may also not be as clearly defined. Using an established typology allowed Spillane to employ a more clearly defined and robust system of categorization.

Having made a strong case for how one might think about learning (paragraphs 3–6), the one remaining step in Spillane's argument is to explain how his study relates different perspectives on learning to implementation outcomes. He has already made the case that it *should* matter, but to fully convince readers of the viability and rigor of the study, he needs to articulate how he went about exploring whether and how it actually did matter. Here the discussion shifts from a theoretical focus (paragraphs 4–6) to a methodological one (paragraphs 7–13).

How you organize research is a function of how you think about a given topic and the kinds of research questions you want to ask. In the SSI study, the primary focus was on how local officials interpreted and thereby constructed policy, and how that process influenced what happened at the school or classroom level. Data collection was organized around this focus. "It was a pretty linear way of thinking," Spillane explained:

> We began with analysis of the state policy environment around mathematics and science. We moved from there to the district, and then the next step was to see what was happening in classrooms. And our hope was that we would learn something about the district from looking at the classrooms. And a lot of that was around the notion of what sense people make would be reflected in district policy, which in turn would influence classroom teachers.

This overarching logic is evident in the description of data collection provided in the article. In paragraphs 7 and 8, Spillane outlines state- and district-level data collection strategies. He describes the logic and process of participant selection, the structure and focus of interviews, and general characteristics of the interviews themselves. As an argument for rigor, these paragraphs accomplish three things. First, they establish that the researcher collected sufficient and appropriate state-level data to understand what the policy was. Second, they establish that the researcher interviewed the appropriate people, given the focus of the study. Third, they emphasize that the questions asked of local officials were general and open-ended; interviews focused on a series of topics but were designed to elicit participants' ideas about mathematics and science reform in their districts. Spillane further signals the study's inductive analytical approach by noting that the second round of interviews was based on preliminary findings from the first round.

In paragraphs 9 and 10, Spillane outlines classroom-level data collection procedures, which included surveys, observations, and interviews. Two purposes are served here. First, he establishes that what he was looking for at the classroom level—implementation of reform-minded instructional practices in mathematics and science—is in fact the outcome of interest. This is an argument for the suitability of the data to the research questions. Second, by describing the sample and the array of data collection strategies used, he indicates the depth and scale at which teacher practice is examined. This is an argument for the credibility of the statements about instruction in the article.

The section of the article on data collection (paragraphs 7–10) seeks to persuade readers that the data collected for the study were both focused on the appropriate topics and substantive enough to generate credible findings. In the paragraphs that follow (11–13), Spillane makes a similar set of arguments about data analysis. The goal is to demonstrate to readers that a clear and rigorous process was employed to explore and define local officials' theories of teacher learning and to examine the relationship between these theories and classroom practice. To accomplish the former, Spillane walks readers through the steps he took to reduce and focus the data on local officials' theories of teacher learning (paragraphs 11 and 12). To address the latter, he outlines how data from multiple sources about teacher practice were consolidated into cases and coded according to the degree to which that practice was consistent with reform-oriented mathematics instruction (paragraph 13).[1]

In sum, Spillane's research design is mapped onto his conceptual framework. He argues that understanding local officials' theories of learning is an important and underexplored aspect of policy implementation. In relation to this driving belief, Spillane lays out a sampling, data collection, and analysis plan that show how he intends to structure the inquiry. He suggests that local theories of teacher change may influence classroom instruction and then

---

[1]The excerpt included in this discussion does not reflect the full account of how Spillane analyzed teachers' instructional practice. Additional discussion of analysis is provided on pages 399–402 of "Local Theories of Teacher Change." We chose not to include this section because the discussion of methods is intertwined with his discussion of findings. Including this section in its entirety was beyond the scope of this chapter. For additional discussion of analysis of instructional practice, please see Spillane (1999, 2002) and Spillane and Zeuli (1999).

outlines how he will tentatively explore this relationship. The data he collects align with the big ideas in his conceptual framework (that is, local officials' understanding of policy and the instructional practices of mathematics teachers). The analysis he conducts refines those data to more specific constructs (aspects of local officials' theories of teacher learning and the presence of specific reform-oriented instructional practices in mathematics) and explores the relationship between them.

## ☆ THE COEVOLUTION OF CONCEPTUAL FRAMEWORKS AND RESEARCH DESIGN

By the time you see them in publication, good conceptual frameworks like the one discussed here appear fully formed. They are comprehensively argued and closely linked with research questions and design. This is helpful for readers, and it lends credibility and clarity to the research. But it also masks the ways in which conceptual frameworks evolve. In most studies, this process is nonlinear and iterative. You consult literature, identify topics and issues you wish to explore, frame arguments, pose questions, design studies—and then the work begins. And in research, "the work" has a tendency to not behave in quite the way you expect. In some cases, you may have misunderstood something fundamental about the topic you hope to study. More often, though, you learn things you did not plan to learn, but that nonetheless change the way you think about your questions or topics. This in turn feeds back into your conceptual framework, which leads to changes in your approach to the research. Those expecting this process to happen in a linear, tidy fashion will soon discover (and, hopefully, come to appreciate) its generative messiness.

"Local Theories of Teacher Change" offers a strong example of how this generative process works. Spillane did not begin the SSI study with the idea that local officials' theories of teacher learning were important; they emerged from a wider set of data focused on how local officials understood (and thus enacted) policy. This led him to focus on questions of how learning happens, which in turn led him back into the literature and toward the Greeno et al. (1996) typology that serves as his theoretical framework for the article. The conceptual framework presented above is the result of that critically reflective and iterative process.

One of the problems with thinking about literature review as an artifact rather than as a process is that it leads you to think of the frameworks that result as being static and the steps that follow as being linear. You conduct a literature review, collect your data, analyze your data, report your results, and discuss the implications of those results. (This remains the dominant publication format in social science journals.) This often leads to the assumption that you have a problem if your findings do not relate precisely back to your literature review. Instead of returning to the literature to puzzle through what might be happening in your data, you may think your study has gone wrong or that you can only report those findings that conform to your existing literature review. This mindset ritualizes the literature review, thereby reducing possibilities borne out of active engagement in the creation process. Instead of strengthening and informing your study, the literature ends up stunting it.

"Local Theories of Teacher Change" developed into an article precisely because conceptual frameworks evolve. For Spillane, this was not a problem but rather a necessary and vital stage in the lifecycle of this—and any—study. As he explained to us,

> On the one hand, you construct a framework that guides your study design and data collection from the outside. I don't think I have . . . ever done a study that that initial frame was sufficient to get me through data analysis and writing. In other words, always, I've come up against, "Well, this framework is inadequate," for some particular aspect. That may be because at the outset, it was too broad to provide this sort of fine-grained analysis that was necessary for a question like this. Or maybe that sometimes I encounter something that I didn't expect I would be writing about in the beginning, but now I'm writing about, and the framework doesn't speak to it explicitly enough. And I think in the case of this article that was the situation. The notion that "the pedagogy of policy" or the notion of "district policymakers as teacher educators," I guess that was . . . there implicitly, but it wasn't an explicit focus, from what I can remember. And instead I think this was something that came up—it looked interesting. I suspect what happened here is that we coded the data first around the category of what is it they think . . . they're thinking about teacher learning and change, and then I needed something to help narrow down and really analyze . . . the data that was coded under that. So this is a good example of a situation where—which again, I think has happened in every study—where there's something else I want to pursue here, and the original framework has limitations as a tool. I need to go back into the literature.

Because conceptual frameworks are closely linked to research design, development in one leads to development in the other. In the case of this article, data collection had already been completed by the time Spillane arrived at theories of teacher learning, so the shift in conceptual framework did not alter that aspect of the study. But it had significant implications for how the data were analyzed. As discussed above, this article is the outgrowth of a shift from an inductive analytical approach to a deductive one. That shift was precipitated by the incorporation of a new theoretical framework (the Greeno et al., 1996, learning typology) into the larger conceptual framework.

## ☆ CONCEPTUAL FRAMEWORKS AND RESEARCH DESIGN: CONCLUDING THOUGHTS

Two basic research questions prompted the analysis that produced "Local Theories of Teacher Change": (1) How do local officials think about teacher learning? (2) What are the implications of local officials' theories of teacher learning for classroom practice? Spillane discovered these questions through the process of working on his data, finding new puzzles, and ultimately returning to the literature to try to figure out those puzzles. It is through this fitting together of previous work and existing research that you come to discover—to excavate from what is already known—new research questions, which in turn inform your thinking about what data to collect and how to analyze those data. In good research, the conceptual frameworks we see in publication present a compelling argument for those questions. But it is the process of developing those frameworks that is most important—a process that is no less than your learning of your topic, in all its complexity, as it unfolds.

## ☆ READING REFERENCES

Anderson, C., & Smith, E. (1987). Teaching science. In V. Richardson-Koehler (Ed.), *Educators' handbook: A research perspective* (pp. 84–111). New York: Longman.

Brown, A. (1978). Knowing when, where, and how to remember: A problem of metacognition. In R. Glaser (Ed.), *Advances in instructional psychology* (pp. 77–165). Hillsdale, NJ: Lawrence Erlbaum.

Cohen, D. K., & Barnes, C. A. (1993). Pedagogy and policy. In D. K Cohen, M. W. McLaughlin, & J. E. Talbert (Eds.), *Teaching for understanding: Challenges for policy and practice* (pp. 207–239). San Francisco: Jossey-Bass.

Confrey, J. (1990). A review of the research on student conceptions in mathematics, science, and programming. In C. Cazden (Ed.), *Review of Research in Education*, Vol. 16. (pp. 3–56). Washington DC: American Educational Research Association.

EEPA. (1990). *Educational Evaluation and Policy Analysis. 12*(3).

Elmore, R. F., & McLaughlin, M. W. (1988). *Steady work: Policy, practice and the reform of American education*. Santa Monica, CA: Rand.

Gagne, R. (1965). *The conditions of learning*. New York: Holt, Rinehart & Winston.

Greeno, J., Collins, A., & Resnick, L. (1996). Cognition and learning. In D. Berliner & R. Calfee (Eds.), *Handbook of educational psychology* (pp. 15–46). New York: Simon & Schuster.

Hutchins, E. (1995a). How a cockpit remembers its speeds. *Cognitive Science, 19,* 265–288.

Hutchins, E. (1995b). *Cognition in the wild.* Cambridge, MA: MIT Press.

Lave, J. (1988). Situating learning in communities of practice. In L. Resnick, S. Levine, & L. Teasley (Eds.), *Perspectives of socially shared cognition* (pp. 63–82). Cambridge, MA: MIT Press.

Lepper, M., & Greene, D. (1979). *The hidden costs of reward.* Hillsdale, NJ: Lawrence Erlbaum.

McDonnell, L. M., & Elmore, R. F. (1987). Getting the job done: Alternative policy instruments. *Educational Evaluation & Policy Analysis, 9*(2), 133–152.

Newell, A., & Simon, H. (1972). *Human problem-solving.* Englewood Cliffs, NJ: Prentice Hall.

Pea, R. (1993). Practices of distributed intelligence and designs for education. In G. Salomon (Ed.), *Distributed cognition: Psychological and educational considerations* (pp. 47–87). New York: Cambridge University Press.

Piaget, J. (1970). *Science of education and the psychology of the child.* New York: Orion Press.

Resnick, L. (1991). Shared cognition: Thinking as social practice. In L. Resnick, J. Levine, & S. Teasley (Eds.), *Perspectives on socially shared cognition* (1–20). Washington, DC: American Psychological Association.

Richardson, V. (1999). Teacher education and the construction of meaning. In G. Griffin (Ed.), *The Education of Teachers, 98*(1). Retrieved from http://nsse-chicago.org/Yearbooks.asp

Schifter, D. (1996). *What's happening in math class? Vol. 2: Reconstructing professional identities.* New York: Teachers College Press.

Spillane, J. P., & Zeuli, J. S. (1999). Reform and mathematics teaching: Exploring patterns of practice in the context of national and state reforms. *Educational Evaluation and Policy Analysis, 21*(1), 1–27.

Vygotsky, L. (1978). *Mind in society: The development of higher psychological processes.* Cambridge, MA: Harvard University Press.

# CHAPTER 4

# THE ROLE OF THE CONCEPTUAL FRAMEWORK IN DATA COLLECTION AND FIELDWORK

A central goal of this book is to clarify and illuminate the role of conceptual frameworks throughout the empirical research process. This chapter focuses on the particular influences and implications of the conceptual framework as it relates to data collection and approaches to fieldwork more broadly. We highlight the close relationship between the arguments that researchers make for a study's relevance and importance and those that we make for its rigor. Simply put, the choices you make about what to study are tightly interwoven with those you make about how to study it. A central purpose of conceptual frameworks is to make both explicit and to provide both you and your audience with a clearly articulated rationale for the methodological choices you make throughout the research process.

Methodology, however, is no simple matter. Both how you think about doing the work and how you carry it out require careful consideration of your role as a researcher, how you see the world (and yourself within it), what to emphasize (and de-emphasize) in your data collection and analysis, and how to represent yourself, your work, and the study's context and participants to your readers. The ways that you wrestle with these complexities shape your conceptual framework at the same time they are shaped by it (Golafshani, 2003; Norris, 1997).

## ☆ WHO YOU ARE, HOW YOU THINK, AND WHAT YOU STUDY

A significant challenge in designing and conducting research is to critically examine and make transparent the goals, commitments, frames of reference, guiding concepts and theories, and working assumptions that influence your work (Anderson & Saavedra, 1995; Chawla, 2006; Peshkin, 1988). In our work teaching and advising students, we often find that they engage in their research as if there is little or no connection between their methods and findings; their own subjectivities, priorities, theoretical orientations; and their design and methods. As Hammersley and Atkinson (2007) argue, researchers must understand that there is an "inseparability of methods and findings, p. " that how one approaches data collection—and, we would add, what one brings to the design and framing of the research as a whole—has much to do with the quality and content of one's data and therefore has a significant influence on one's analyses and findings (Peshkin, 1988; Ravitch & Wirth, 2007). But what does this mean operationally? How can you conceptualize and then analyze these relationships, and use that understanding to make better choices about methodology? How do your guiding assumptions, commitments (theoretical and political), belief systems, relationship to the participants and setting, and conceptual framing of the research topic and focal populations of your research influence the various components and dimensions of your fieldwork?

Focusing on "Theorizing Hyphenated Selves: Researching Youth Development in and Across Contentious Political Contexts," by Michelle Fine and Selcuk Sirin, in this chapter we center our discussion on the relationship between conceptual frameworks and data collection and fieldwork. Fine is an internationally recognized qualitative researcher specializing in participatory action research and other applied qualitative methodologies that sit at the intersection of psychology, education, and sociology. She is known for taking her research to places—literally and figuratively—where few are willing or able to go, working in deeply participatory ways with socially marginalized groups such as out-of-school youth and incarcerated women. Most important for our purposes, Fine is a sophisticated thinker about the close relationship between what we study and how we study it. She does not see herself as an observer of social and political situations, as many researchers do, but as an actor in those situations. Similarly, the conduct of research in Fine's view is anything but value neutral. As the article discussed in this chapter shows, Finc argucs that people's assumptions about what is "normal" or "objective" serve to legitimize or validate some groups or behaviors while marginalizing others. In challenging these assumptions, she also interrogates how they are produced—a process that leads back to questioning the role of research and of herself as a researcher. Bourdieu's (1989, 1990) concept of people as embodied histories helps us to understand Fine's reflexive stance on herself as an instrument of the research. For Fine, any inquiry into a social process or phenomenon is also an inquiry into one's self. Her ability to conceptualize, articulate, and methodologically address how her own history and ideological beliefs influence her research—both what she chooses to explore and how she structures those explorations—has allowed her to break new ground both theoretically and methodologically.

In this chapter, we first discuss the intellectual background and context for "Theorizing Hyphenated Selves." We then present excerpts from the article itself, as well as a second publication (by the same authors) that articulates more fully the wider conceptual terrain within which the article can be located. Following the excerpts, we summarize Fine and Sirin's argument and analyze the relationship between how the argument was framed and how the data were collected. We focus specifically on how the conceptual framework for this research was developed, the relationship between the topic of the study and the stance of the researchers, and in turn how that stance informed specific choices about data collection. We conclude with a discussion of the iterative, ever-evolving nature of conceptual frameworks as they are developed, challenged, and refuted through engaging reflexively in fieldwork.

## ABOUT THE AUTHOR ☆

Michelle Fine is Distinguished Professor of Social Psychology, Women's Studies, and Urban Education at the Graduate Center of the City University of New York. Lewinian with a twist, Fine's work braids social psychological theory with feminist and critical race theory, participatory methods, and strong commitments to social change. Fine has authored or coauthored numerous "classics" within justice studies, including books and articles on high school dropouts, women with disabilities, the "missing discourse of desire" in sex education classrooms, Muslim-American youth, participatory action research methods, and the impact of college on women in prison.

A pioneer in the field of youth participatory action research (PAR), Fine has been involved with a series of participatory studies by youth and elders, from across different racial, ethnic, and social class backgrounds, within "contact zones" to investigate the contours of exclusion, oppression, and violations of dignity and to generate strategies for youth-based resistance and possibility. With teams of elders and youth, Fine and colleagues have created a variety of products, including policy documents, spoken-word performances, youth websites, scholarly documents, and historic accounts of struggles for human rights across prisons, schools, and communities.

As a much-sought-after expert witness in gender and race discrimination education cases, Fine's research and testimony have been most influential in the victories of women who sued for access to The Citadel military academy in South Carolina and in *Williams v. California*, a class action lawsuit on behalf of urban youth of color denied adequate education in California. Most recently Fine and a PAR team, including women from Bedford Hills Correctional Facility, published *Changing Minds: The Impact of College in a Maximum-Security Prison* (2001), which is nationally recognized as the primary empirical basis for the contemporary college-in-prison movement.

The national and international recognition of her work is evident in a sampling of recent awards, which include the 2008 Social Justice Award from the Cross Cultural Winter Roundtable, the 2007 Willystine Goodsell Award from the American Educational Research Association, the 2005 First Annual Morton Deutsch Award, an honorary doctoral degree in education and social justice from Bank Street College in 2002, and the Carolyn Sherif Award from the American Psychological Association in 2001.

## ☆ BACKGROUND AND CONTEXT: AN OVERVIEW OF THE WORK IN FOCUS

Like most people, researchers studying child and adolescent development tend to think of it in individualized terms. *Development* implies change, but the change is often assumed to be occurring largely *inside* the young person. The wider social environment in which the change is unfolding is seen as a backdrop, if it is seen at all.

Sometimes, though, the background changes so radically that persons can be seen and treated completely differently one day than they were the day before—a change that has profound developmental implications. Such was the case for Muslim-American youth before and after the events of September 11, 2001. Beyond its intrinsic value and narrative power, their story is important because the disruption and reframing of the identities of this group of young people says a lot about the wider society of the United States and the power structures in which their lives and experiences are framed and embedded.

Telling this story, however, is not easy. How do researchers and those involved in youth development more broadly go about gaining an understanding of how youth construct their identities—specifically, when youth hail from marginalized groups in socially and politically contentious contexts? How can we understand the tensions and crosscurrents in youths' social, psychological, and academic development, given all the moving parts of their identities and the social, political, familial, and institutional contexts that shape them?

Further, if one's research seeks to investigate the influences of power, hegemony, and inequity on identity development with marginalized and oppressed populations, one's research methods must interrupt broad social trends that serve to marginalize the voices of these research participants given the power structures and how they become instantiated and enacted within the research process itself. This represents a significant challenge. More often than not, researchers are employed by (and therefore a part of) the very institutions whose construction of these populations has reinforced their marginalized status. It is a tension not easily resolved.

The work of Michelle Fine sits at these disciplinary, theoretical, and ideological crossroads. Fine's research has embedded into its design the multiply situated theoretical, ideological, and methodological concepts and approaches necessary to investigate and understand the shifting terrain of adolescent identity construction and the personal, social, familial, and institutional influences on these intra- and interpsychic processes. To traverse this conceptual, theoretical, relational, and interdisciplinary terrain, researchers need framing concepts that seek complexity and hybridization rather than status quo and normative understandings of the phenomena in focus. Within this conceptual milieu, the concept of *hyphenated identities* has become central to Fine's empirical work because it allows for a kind of conceptual and methodological innovation that rests upon deeply considered social critique that hails from, as it crosses over, disciplines and fields. Fine's work adds layers of complexity to discourses on youth identity development because of its conceptual complexity and richness as well as because of the generative tensions between its theoretical frames and methodological considerations.

Across Fine's career as a researcher, the concept of the hyphen—as a marker and symbol of an active, highly individualized meaning-making and identity formation process that both invokes and involves complex social and political forces—is a thread she weaves into a broader framework of and approach to critical, reflexive, and relational research. The hyphen is both metaphorical and analytical. It is a framing concept that allows Fine to argue for a rigorous methodological approach that shows fidelity to the complexity of people's lives and identities rather than a dogmatic adherence to methods that is so often the norm in research (Harrison, MacGibbon, & Morton, 2001). She urges researchers to view all people—not only those in positions of power—as meaning makers and experts concerning their own experiences (Brooks & Davies, 2007; Liiv, 1998), to examine how aspects of people's identities intersect with larger social and political forces to create identity responses that are complex and difficult to neatly typologize (Ravitch, 2000). Fine's work calls for research to be interpersonally authentic and respectfully critical of mainstream views that essentialize, reduce, and oversimplify the lives of research participants (as well as researchers), especially those who are socially and politically marginalized.

The idea of the hyphen as a metaphor both for social processes or phenomena and for the research process itself has long been a theme in Michelle Fine's work. Its genesis is both biographical and intellectual, constituted by multiple influences (disciplinary, conceptual, relational, and lived experience) while at the same framing her way of conceptualizing new problems and contexts. In an interview that focused on her work, Fine stated, "The way I think about all research is that it's driven by biography, theory, desire, and context." She explained:

That is, *hyphenated selves*, as a notion, comes easily to me, biographically, because I have an enormous amount of discomfort in any space that I feel is calling for homogeneity or monogamy in commitments, and I am, by style, probably most comfortable in places where questions of difference are at play, and up for grabs. There's something about what would be called *essentialism* that not only offends me intellectually, but scares me, personally. So, the strands that help me get there are, I am, both my parents are Jewish-Polish immigrants from Poland, although they would never say "Polish," it was just a stop through, to schlep through, to be treated like shit through, to get out the other end through, and my mom who's now 95 is the youngest of 18 kids. . . . My dad sells plumbing supplies. And getting invited to the [university] president's house and not knowing which fork to use. And so, I'm interested in the hyphens we all live on. I actually find them both a source of my anxiety and my best thinking. And so I think hyphenated selves, coming out of the Muslim-American work, has a longer trajectory in my own body.

As this vignette illustrates, Fine relates her personal background to the ways that she engages in research; she works in focused ways to locate herself as a shaper of the values, lenses, and conditions of the research. But the concept of the hyphen is not solely a product of Fine's personal story. It also provides her with a useful way of thinking about identity construction, a central theme in all of her work. For Fine, the concept of hyphenated selves allows for a complexity of understanding of people's perspectives on their own identity construction, and resists hegemonic understandings and representations of underserved and marginalized populations. In describing her early work with high school dropouts, Fine described the evolution of her own thinking about hyphenated selves.

> I remember when I was exploring *Framing Dropouts* [Fine, 1991], I just kept interviewing smart kids who had dropped out. . . . So I think of that in light of a lot of my work with kids who have been pushed out of school, or women in prison, that there's a kind of, another whole knowledge that's going on. . . . So, I think it was between self and other, and . . . I think in all of those settings I've been working this question of, "To what extent do our methods reproduce our fantasies of the *other* rather than interrogate the complexity of our own privileged point of view and the complexity of people who have been deemed *others?*"

In this statement, Fine complicates the relationship between the self and "other" as a means of resisting a pejorative, hegemonically framed perspective on what *other* means. This is a recursive cycle of thought, reflection, and action—she intentionally works at this intersection of concept and method as a response to her beliefs about what it means to engage with people in a true exploration into aspects of their lives and the conditions in which their perceptions and social identities are formed and reformed over time.

To best understand the conceptual framework upon which "Theorizing Hyphenated Selves" is built, it is helpful to consider the larger study from which this article emerged. In 2003, Fine and several colleagues began exploratory research with Muslim-American youth about their identity development during the period before and after the attacks on the United States on September 11, 2001. In formulating and then carrying out the study, they developed the idea of *hyphenated selves* as a theoretical framework (our term) to explain the dynamic process of identity construction in complicated and even fraught political and social contexts. Specifically, the study examined the intra- and interpersonal identity negotiations among Muslim-American youth in the wake of dramatic shifts in American public opinion of Muslims following the events of September 11. While Muslim-American youth were previously made the object of what Fine and others refer to as an "orientalizing gaze," they had been nonetheless seen as relatively "ordinary" in an ethnic American landscape. After September 11, Muslim-Americans found quickly that their social positioning had changed and they were suddenly subjected to suspicion, surveillance, hostility, and violence. In a separate article, Sirin and Fine (2007, pp. 151–152) advanced an argument for the importance of this topic:

[1] Adolescence is a developmental period during which young people form, and then reform, their cultural identities (Erikson, 1980; Fine & Torre, 2004; Fine, Burns, Payne & Torre, 2004; Helms, 1990; Solis, 2003; Way & Robinson, 2003). This may be a particularly complex psychological task for youth living in contexts, or historic moments, in which their diverse racial, ethnic, national, religious, sexual origins stir in tension (Willis, 2002). When one's social identity is fiercely contested by the dominant discourse either through formal institutions, social relationships, and/or the media, one of the first places we can witness psychological, social and political fallout is in the lives of young people. As Willis (2002) suggests, youth embody and perform the very economic, and we would add cultural, conflicts that constitute global politics. Adolescence is precisely the moment in which international, national, social and personal "crises" erupt most publicly and spontaneously, and, unfortunately, they are more often than not misread as simply personal, hormonal, disciplinary or developmental "problems" (Abu El-Haj, 2005; Appadurai, 2004; Fine et al., 2004; Sen, 2004; Sirin, Diemmer, Jackson, Gonsalves, & Howell, 2004; Sirin & Rogers-Sirin, 2005). Growing up in the midst of what Fazal Rizvi (2005) calls Islamophobia, Muslim American youth offer us a lens into the developmental challenges that confront teens who live on the intimate fault lines of global conflict; teens who carry international crises in their backpacks and in their souls.

[2] For Muslim youth living in the US, negotiating their identities across different cultural terrains became decidedly more challenging after the events of 9/11 (Cainkar, 2004). On one hand, their lives, like those of everyone else in the U.S., were under attack. On the other hand, they were perceived as a potential threat to the safety of their neighbors. Ideologically represented as a threat, since 9/11 "they"—Muslim Americans—have been watched, detained, deported, and invaded in order to protect and save "us." Just as life in their 'home countries' erupted in international and domestic conflict, these youth and their families came to be perceived as potential threats to U.S. national security. This situation did not dissipate after the initial attacks of 9/11, but rather, it continues today, reinforced every time there is news of a security threat. At this moment in history in the United States these young people are at once becoming more

religiously grounded and nationally rootless; transnational yet homeless (Bhabha, 2005; Levitt, 2000).

[3] Since 9/11, we have learned much about the U.S. attitudes toward Muslims and other cultures (see Gerges, 2003), but the developmental consequences for youth of a world fractured by religious terror and global conflicts have yet to be determined, particularly for Muslim youth upon whom the heaviest burden may lie—at least in the U.S. We take seriously young people's experiences of witnessing and critically speaking back to global, national, cultural and economic contradictions (Fine, Roberts, Torre, Bloom, Burns, Chajet, Guishard, & Payne, 2004), and believe they bring passion, loss, desire and critical action to ongoing, shifting cultural formations. It is our view that these young women and men offer a theoretical lens on many groups of youth who struggle with economic/cultural oppression, hegemonic representations of self (Deaux & Philogone, 2001; Solis, 2003) and diminished opportunities for selfhood in the post 9/11 U.S. context.

[4] In our efforts to build a conceptual framework that can guide our study, given the paucity of specific research on Muslim Americans, we gained insights from three areas of related research on immigrant minority youth. Research on immigrant youth shows that the successful integration of both one's own culture and the dominant culture, leads to more positive developmental outcomes (Berry, 1997; Berry & Kim, 1988; Nesdale, Rooney, & Smith, 1997; Oppedal, Røysamb, & Sam, 2004; Oppedal, Røysamb, & Heyerdahl, 2005; Phinney, Cantu, & Kurtz, 1997) whereas marginalization, that is disengagement from both cultures, is associated with mental health problems for immigrant youth. Previous research on minority youth in general (e.g., Fisher, Wallace, & Fenton, 2000; Lorenzo, Frost, & Reinherz, 2000; Romero & Roberts, 2003), and immigrant youth in particular (e.g., Berry, 1997; Nesdale, Rooney, & Smith, 1997; Suarez-Orozco, 2005), also show strong evidence that minority stress (i.e., discrimination and stress associated with one's social status) can lead to mental health problems in terms of depression, anxiety, and psychosomatic complaints. Thus, the developmental process for immigrant youth not only originates from the challenges of reconciling multiple cultural systems of reference but also from discrimination and stress due to one's minority status (LaFramboise, Coleman, & Gerton, 1993).

[5] Further, drawing theoretically from the writings of Amartya Sen (2004), we also recognize that culture is but one aspect of self, flowing in interaction with other complex dimensions of selfhood; that culture

is "not a homogeneous attribute" (43) but rather is filled with the tensions and delights of discordance; that "culture absolutely does not sit still," (43) and that "cultures interact with each other and cannot be seen as insulated structures." (44). We add to Sen's working definition by noting that when a culture is under siege, it becomes particularly prominent for those who live within the diaspora, like immigrant Muslims in the U.S. The social and psychological tensions are exacerbated when home countries shatter in conflict, when one's culture is hijacked by terrorists, and when one's new country marks you as suspect. In times of tension and conflict, as Yuval-Davis (2001) notes, cultural binaries and oppositions proliferate. The intense stereotyping and dehumanization of Muslims in the U.S. reflects this dynamic poignantly. It is in the very sinews of adolescent lives that we come to see how culture and global politics enter the body and soul of U.S. youth (see Rao & Walton, 2004).

"Theorizing Hyphenated Selves" builds upon this argument, but focuses more explicitly on how the concept of hyphenated selves should be studied. Using our own definition of a conceptual framework, the article takes as its starting point that the topic is important, and delves deeply into an argument for why the methods used were appropriate—even necessary—given the subject matter. As such, the article embodies the central theme of this chapter: the close relationship between what you choose to study and how you go about studying it. Because we have already extensively quoted the authors about the rationale for studying this topic, we have selected the excerpt below to focus on their discussion of how they went about doing so. We then highlight the various ways that the larger conceptual framework for the study informed both the authors' conceptualization of the research process and the actual work of data collection.

Fine, M., & Sirin, S. R. (2007). Theorizing hyphenated selves: Researching youth development in and across contentious political contexts. *Social and Personality Psychology Compass*, *1*, 1–23; Reprinted by permission of the publisher (Taylor & Francis Group, http://www.informaworld.com).

## Methods for Studying Hyphenated Selves

[6] We took up an intensive investigation of the hyphen, theorized as a dynamic social psychological space where political arrangements and individual subjectivities meet. We came to understand that the psychological texture of the hyphen is substantially informed by history, media, surveillance, politics, nation of origin, gender, biography,

longings, imagination, and loss—whether young people know/speak this or not. Across maps, interviews, and surveys, we could see great variety in young peoples' experiences of self/selves, Others and how they negotiated the hyphen in distinct contexts—on a bus, in an airport, at the dinner table, at school and in the mosque. While some spoke of the hyphen as a solid wall of mistrust, others describe it as a porous membrane. . . . Some portray the hyphen as a traumatic check point, and others as a space for cautious collaboration, public education, or (as you will see below) assertive confrontation. For a few it is a space of shame, for many a site of anxiety and for others an opportunity to invent new versions of self. (p. 6)

[7] The hyphenated selves approach is not, however, simply a conceptual framework. It also carries methodological implications. If researchers are to situate young lives in and across historic, cultural, and political contexts; link narratives of identity to distant and local political arrangements and interrogate intersectionality and wide variability within the "group," we confront questions of design (see Shohat, 2006). . . . We reflect here on the methodological choices we have made toward understanding the complexity of the hyphen, even as we remain skeptical and humble always about these decisions, all too aware of their limitations, their ambitions, and the impossibility of "catching politics" as they circulate through the rapidly metabolizing bodies of youth. (p. 8)

[8] We gathered a diverse group of Muslim youth, ages 12 to 18, from the New York and New Jersey area, with varied experiences and standpoints, to help us refine the research questions, articulate the design and the methods, and think about the ethics of research on/ with politically vulnerable young people. By design, participatory action research (PAR) projects rest on the assumption that social research should be sculpted through the knowledge carried by young people and adults most intimately affected by injustice and struggle. (pp. 8–9)

[9] [The youth] helped us create a design of mixed methods—surveys, focus groups, mapping, individual life stories—to best capture complex and layered stories about Muslim-American youth individually and collectively, as they matured amid the post-9/11 "war on terror" political context. They warned us about ethical concerns, critiqued traditional measures of stress and youth "risk" behaviors, laughed at the "dating measures" we thought about using and gently educated us. (p. 9)

*On mixing the methods*

[10]  Methodologically, we tried to develop a research design that could stretch to uncover the layered complexity of youth growing up in politically contentious contexts, including qualitative and quantitative information constructed by individuals and groups, about processes that are very much on their mind and buried in their personal and collective unconscious, documenting how local conditions and distant arrangements effect stories of self and relations with others. And then we sought to generate an analytic plan that would allow us to review the data by gender, nation of origin, parents' educational level, heterogeneity of community, type of school, religiosity, etc. While a theory of hyphenated selves may appear to be most compatible with qualitative methods, we have found ourselves interested in intentionally mixing qualitative and quantitative methods. (p. 10)

[11]  [W]e gathered a sample of more than 200 youth from across communities (primarily New York and New Jersey, but also a few from across the USA) and asked them to construct maps, participate in focus groups, sit for interviews and complete surveys consisting of a number of open-ended questions and a set of psychometrically validated measures. Given the developmental shifts in identity formation, we sampled youth in two age cohorts (12–18 and 18–25) who completed quantitative surveys that assessed multiple social and cultural identifications with "Muslim communities" and "mainstream US society,"[1] their experiences of and responses to discrimination, and standardized measures of psychological well-being and health. The survey also, at the encouragement of our youth advisory group, included questions about the books they are reading, stresses in their lives from family and school, and imaginative open-ended questions asking them what messages they would include in an MTV show about Muslim-American teens. Our mixed design allowed us to document common experiences of Muslim-American youth but also to excavate the rich variation of and within this group of young people. Via surveys we were able to generate descriptive statistics and correlations between discrimination and strength of ethnic identity that help us situate some of

---

[1]Both extremely problematic—from our perspective—categorizations were accepted at the insistence of our PAR advisory board, who explained that even though all of the respondents are from the USA, they do not always identify as "American."

the experiences of Muslim-American youth alongside other marginalized groups and to articulate a theory of how unequal power relations affect youth development. At the same time, with interviews, maps, and open-ended questions we were able to go beyond the most typical experiences and understand the rich variation within this group of young people, in their own words/drawings. In addition to learning from each method one at a time, we also combined various aspects of these multiple methods through research questions. For example, in order to examine how young people negotiate their hyphenated selves, we produced cross-tabulations of survey responses by three metacodes of the maps: evidence of integrated lives at the hyphen, evidence of parallel lives, and evidence of conflict and tension between lives. The results from this mixing of the methods not only answered our research question but also validated the new method (the maps in this case) with previously established survey measures. Our point here is simple: the theory of hyphenated selves has implications not only for conceptual framing but also for design, methods, and analysis. (pp. 10–11)

[12] In our work with varied groups of youth in schools, communities, juvenile facilities and with the Muslim-American teens, we have relied on an old social-psychological method—long buried and deserving of resuscitation—the personal "identity map." Variations of this projective method have psychoanalytic roots with Winnicott, Winnicott, and Shepard and Davis (1989) and have been applied by environmental psychologists (Lynch, 1960; Saarinen, 1973), radical geographers (Geiseking, 2007; Hart, 1981; Harvey, 2001; Katz, 2003), and social psychologists, most notably Milgram and Jodelet (1976).

[13] While the prompts may vary depending on the research project—draw the city, your selves, safe and dangerous spaces in your life, a conflict in your life, your journey to your new country or into the future—across projects young people take the invitation for creativity and run with it. With the Muslim-American youth, we asked them simply to draw their selves (i.e., student, daughter/son, athlete, Muslim, American [see Figure 4.1]) the way they see it. We gave them crayons, markers, paper, and about 15 minutes. We have collected, to date, more than 200 of these maps, which reveal, as Willis would suggest, the varied ways in which young lives connect to political events, social arrangements, religious and cultural traditions, mass media and youth culture, interpersonal relationships, personal yearnings and fears, fantasies about home country and the USA. p.

**Figure 4.1** Youth map: Documenting layers of self

[14] We also used surveys to assess how young people negotiate their identities as Muslim-Americans. In order to avoid creating—and measuring—a false dichotomy, that is, creating a framework that forces the research participants to pick one identity over another, we allowed for the possibility of having two unrelated identifications. Superficially, in our

surveys we created parallel forms where in one set of questions we measured the degree to which young people identify with Muslim communities using the collective self-esteem measure (Luhtanen & Crocker, 1992) and an additional form where we used the same set of questions to capture the degree of identification with mainstream US society. Unlike more typical survey items where the participants are asked to choose their location in a bidirectional continuum (i.e., Muslim-American) or even worse, choosing one or the other, we asked them to rate each identity independently. It is possible, of course, that the two forms reified the distinctions between these identities, particularly for those seeking "fusion" selves, but with this measurement strategy we were able to directly test the now famous "clash of civilization" hypothesis to see how compatible these two forms of identifications [were]. Surveying the hyphen in this way also allowed us to create psychological models of what might be called critical pluralism, understanding the bases of "Muslim collective identity" and the bases of "Mainstream US collective identity." (pp. 13–14)

[15]   After youth completed surveys and maps, a subset were invited to participate in focus groups. Here we could interrogate, for example, the meaning of the red core, the source of the questions, the weight of external influences and what enables and threatens the balance, in the maps displayed above. As Wilkinson (1999) and Wilkinson and Kitzinger (1995, 2000, 2003) have argued in their now classic essays on focus groups and conversational analysis, focus groups enable researchers to connect understandings of selves-in-relation with analyses of how young people actually engage with, experience, and perform in live *social settings*. Focus groups offer social spaces where "differences" are animated and contact is engaged; where researchers can witness the intersubjective performances of self, distancing from, projections onto and alliances and confrontations with others. (p. 14)

[16]   Maps and focus groups offer up interpretive material, therefore, that can be analyzed with respect for the material presented as it is, but also with an analytic eye for what is absent; enabling researchers to analyze at once, *what is* but also *what is not said*. (p. 16)

## THE ARGUMENT ☆

In Sirin and Fine's 2007 article (paragraphs 1–5), the authors articulate a clear rationale for studying identity development among Muslim-American youth in the post–September 11 era. "Theorizing Hyphenated Selves" focuses on the methodological implications of that choice. As such, the argument takes a different turn, focused on persuading the reader that the choice of topic and research questions necessitates a different set of methodological considerations. It opens with a note that this is conceptually challenging terrain, and that any methodological choice about how to study it involves concessions and trade-offs (paragraphs 6 and 7). There is an inherent tension here: The authors are at once trying to convince the reader to follow them into unfamiliar (and perhaps uncomfortable) terrain, while acknowledging that there may be intellectual, social, and political risks involved. This dualism—in which Fine seeks more compelling ways to define the world while remaining suspicious of her role in doing so—is a recurrent theme in her work. The methodology she and her coauthor then outline is an outgrowth of Fine's years of critical engagement in PAR. Fine has chosen (and refined) a PAR approach because it seeks to create a dynamic, generative, level playing field of communication and interaction between researchers and participants in ways that guide and support each phase of data collection to be as democratic and exploratory as possible. Such an approach was especially important for the present study, Fine explained:

> [PAR] just insists that that knowledge is at the table, and helps shaping the questions, and the methods, and the design, and the interpretation. . . . So, I think it went from an epistemology/methodology thing—like, how do we design our research so we're not reproducing othering—to understanding the veil and the performances of identities, particularly in groups that have been marginalized.

Having positioned themselves as a part of the research, the authors then show how this positioning, combined with their choice of topic, shaped their methodological choices. As an argument, the goal is to show how specific aspects of their methodology reflect the position described above. As such, it is framed in terms of choices about research design overall, as well as specific data collection strategies:

1. To guard against making Muslim-American youth an object of research, participants were engaged in decision making about what kinds of data to collect and how to collect it (paragraphs 8 and 9).

2. Because the participants were diverse, data collection and analysis strategies sought to draw out the individual nuances of their stories and experiences while allowing for cross-sectional or comparative analyses. Therefore, a mixed methods design combining surveys with various qualitative techniques was most appropriate (paragraphs 10 and 11).

3. Identity construction is both personal (individually nuanced) and relational (set against the backdrop of community, family, society, and culture), and consists of both explicit and tacit aspects of one's sense of self. For this reason, identity maps were used to anchor qualitative data collection (paragraphs 12 and 13).

4. To ensure that surveys did not force respondents into categories that were artificially neat or dichotomous, surveys were designed to allow for multiple identifications (paragraph 14).

5. To explain and gain depth on the identity maps, they were discussed with participants in focus groups. Focus groups were chosen because of their social, interactive, and performative nature, allowing researchers to observe as well as listen to explanations of identity construction (paragraph 15).

In the sections that follow, we first discuss the evolutionary and iterative nature of conceptual frameworks, focusing on how the idea of hyphenated selves evolved into a theoretical framework in Fine's work. We then turn to a fuller exploration of the links between conceptual frameworks and data collection in that work, focusing on three critical aspects in the process: stance, design, and modes of data collection. We conclude with a brief discussion of the nature and meaning of rigor in Fine's methodology, and how it is informed by her conceptual framework.

Before delving more deeply into the article itself, it is important to note that in both the article quoted above (paragraph 4) and when interviewed, Fine uses the term *conceptual framework* somewhat differently than we do in this book. Specifically, her working definition is more along the lines of what we term a *theoretical framework*; that is, a crafting together of theories (paragraphs 1–5) to illuminate a particular topic, problem, or phenomenon. As we noted in Chapter 1, the labels are less important than the definitions. For the remainder of this chapter, when Fine and Sirin refer to *hyphenated selves* as a conceptual framework, we will quote them as such. In our own analysis, however, we will continue to use the terms *conceptual* and *theoretical framework* in accordance with the definitions presented in Chapter 1.

## *HYPHENATED SELVES* AS A ☆ THEORETICAL FRAMEWORK

The concept of hyphenated selves developed over more than twenty years of Fine's research with and across various marginalized groups. In recursive fashion, it includes reflection on how her own background influences how she constructs research—that is, her process of creating the most expansive possible set of concepts for use as investigative tools and analytic frames. Throughout her research, the voices, realities, needs, imposed constraints, and possibilities of participants are a central aspect of Fine's engagement across populations and settings (paragraphs 7–10). Fine's research with Muslim-American youth exemplifies how conceptual frameworks can be both actively developed and still developing. Her conceptual framework is both formed and porous; it is a foundation to the research even as it remains actively open to the learnings from the work as it unfolds.

While the idea of hyphenated selves grew out of Fine's own work, it did not develop in a vacuum. Like all research, Fine's research joins a conversation already underway—a conversation that she found in many ways troubling. "One thing that was important for us early on was to think about audience," she explained.

> We were writing on a contentious issue: a group of young people, who were seen as the potential bodies for either patriotism or terrorism or oppression who then became terrorists pretty quickly [post-9/11]. So we weren't writing in a vacuum. . . . So thinking about entering contentious audiences is a little like Double Dutch jump rope. . . . You know, it's hard to figure out when to go in, when's it safe? So, we really had to think about the first hyphen of, for me, who am I? . . . So, the conceptual framework forced me, us, to think about history as a method. And then to figure out which history are we placing them in. . . . So, putting them in the history of exiled youth, and the developmental consequences of being exiled, was a really important theoretical move that I think, for your readers, it's important. . . . And that has everything to do with how you choose your literature review. . . . Every study on Muslims up until that point—Muslim kids—was about *hijab*. You know, just like, the fetish. So, we weren't going to reproduce the fetish. . . . And so, figuring out what argument you want to be making is really important. And then, people have to figure out, does the literature reinscribe a dominant literature, or does it help you make a different argument?

This statement helps elucidate Fine's perspective on a central argument that her and Sirin's research with Muslim-American youth makes: how one can investigate politically, socially, and interpersonally charged topics with marginalized populations in ways that do justice to the complexities that exist within individuals and groups, and how researchers (particularly those who are members of dominant groups) must work through challenges of discerning and confronting hegemonic undercurrents that influence their research choices. Fine and Sirin's research with Muslim-American youth critically examines prior research across several disciplines in order to explore how to situate their research so that it might question or challenge the dominance of less critical research on (not with) Muslim-American youth (paragraphs 3–5). Fine and Sirin propose the concept of hyphenated selves as a new theoretical framework (again, our term) "to better understand youth identity in and across contentious political contexts" (p. 1).

Having explicated the theoretical foundations of the hyphenated selves framework, Fine and Sirin then turn to the methodological implications and challenges of such a framework, and reflect on some of the lessons they have learned from operationalizing it in their own work. In the discussion that follows, we focus on the intersections between the concept of hyphenated selves and the methodological approach of this work, elucidating the ways that the conceptual framework informs, as it is shaped by, one's methodological approach.

## THE HYPHEN AS METHOD: ☆ POSITIONALITY AND PRACTICE

The framing of the hyphenated selves concept instantiates itself in the design of the research, and necessitates a critical attention to data collection. As such, Fine and Sirin's framing of the issues at play with Muslim-American youth—issues of a shifting political, social, and psychological landscape that has both external and internal implications for their social and identity development—requires that they utilize multiple, intersecting methodologies within a participatory mode of inquiry, engaging the participants in the construction of the data collection methods by asking for their authentic, in-depth feedback at the outset and throughout the data collection process (paragraphs 7–9).

One of the most interesting aspects of Fine's research with Muslim-American youth is how the concept of hyphenated selves has roots in, and provides nourishment to, her methodological approach. Her reflexive stance became infused in her methodology, leading to the development and testing of methods that allowed for transparency and approachability of complexity with participants.

Somewhere between epistemology and reflexivity and design lies the question of "How do you think about the relationship between you, your work, the audiences you're speaking to, and the participants you're working with?" And I think this hyphen idea is vibrant at each of those junctures. It's like relational therapy was a departure from psychoanalysis. I think the hyphen illuminates the relational ways in which we do our work. . . . Those of us who are doing critical work have a real obligation to try to make sure that the work doesn't get caught in the undertow of hegemonic representations. And so, kind of at every level now, I think—for me at least—the hyphen gives us pause and courage at the same time.

This approach is in part a result of Fine's interrogation of traditional research methods and an ensuing acknowledgment of their limitations in terms of creating the conditions necessary for participants to have a sense of agency and voice in the research. Her realization of the theoretical and methodological constraints of mainstream research ultimately led Fine to adopt (and adapt) participatory methods, which allowed for greater authenticity, agency, and complexity within the research itself. This process reflects the intertwined nature of theory and methods. Fine's unease with the binary distinctions that exist on either side of the hyphen paralleled her skepticism about the capacity of traditional research methods to complicate those distinctions. Using participatory methods offered a space and an opportunity to wrestle with these complexities.

A conceptual framework is, like, an intellectual, political, and aesthetic experience, right? But it presumes scholarship and politics are constructed, not passive, not flat, not the next question on the horizon. And, I mean, it's really why I love PAR. Because we can create what Maria Torre would call *contact zones*. And then we have to figure out, okay, so if we don't write the story of high schools from the point of view of the principal, or the black boy in the AP class, from whose point of view? . . . And what happens if you actually try to broker different kinds of knowledges?

It is this position of the researcher as a "broker" of knowledge that gives rise to both innovation and complexity in Fine and Sirin's methodology, and that brings to the fore the hyphenated nature of their own roles in relationship to their participants, setting, and topic. On the one hand, they seek to deeply involve Muslim-American young people—the focal population of their research—into the process of data analysis and interpretation. At the same time, however, they remain aware of their own disciplinary backgrounds and institutions, which they ultimately speak back to in their work. The result is a methodology that is itself "hyphenated" in the sense that it simultaneously utilizes and critiques specific techniques for both collecting and analyzing data.

As we argued in Chapter 1, an important function of conceptual frameworks is that they allow you to make reasoned, defensible decisions about your methods. Thus far in this chapter, we have attended closely to the relationship between how the authors conceptualized the topic of their study and their role and position as researchers of that topic. We now turn to the conduct of the research itself, with particular attention to the relationship between the authors' conceptual framework and the data collection strategies employed.

Having arrived at a sense of their stance as researchers and how it related to their conceptual framework, the authors faced the considerable challenge of finding a way to conduct the research in a way that reflected that stance. A guiding premise for the entire process was that the methodology should be transparent. (Indeed, the very publication of "Theorizing Hyphenated Selves" could be seen as an effort to make methodology transparent.) The goal, Fine explained, was to make clear how methodological decisions were made, given the complexity of the topic and positions of the researchers.

> I think it's self-conscious insofar as we try to be very transparent. That is, listing as much as possible the small decisions we've made. Because especially with qualitative work, it feels like that's not done a lot, and it just looks like magic.

The first step in doing so was to think about how the data collection should be designed: what questions should be asked, how, in what order, and in what contexts. It was important for Fine and her colleagues to engage in this work collaboratively with the study participants. They were concerned that a less participatory, person-centered approach would not do justice to the complexities of these young people's lives and therefore, given her values and priorities, would not be an acceptable means of engaging in the research. To that end, Fine and Sirin introduce the study's methodology by noting the critical role played by young people in developing and refining questions, themes, and instruments (paragraphs 8 and 9). A central belief that guides Fine and Sirin's argument about the need for participatory research is that the youth themselves must be given room to actively challenge the researchers' potentially sedimented, biased perspectives, and to do so they need to be viewed and engaged with as experts of their own lives and of their own situated meaning making. In order to inquire into young Muslim-Americans' processes of meaning making about their identities given the contentious milieux into which their lives and the research falls, the youth themselves needed to complicate the theoretical constructs Fine and Sirin brought into the research and how they should approach the inquiry.

> It was clear to me/us that this would have to have to be, even mildly participatory, that the young people would have to help shape the questions

we would ask, the analysis we would undertake, the language we would use. Most of my work at this point is highly participatory. And I don't just do that because I'm a "Leftie," or because I think it's nice, or because I like having seven thousand people's names on articles. But I do it for . . . reasons of what might be called validity. The two places that I enter this are expert validity and construct validity. I do think expertise is distributed. I don't think legitimacy is, but I think expertise is, and I would like to do research with the richest version of expertise possible. And, I think that our constructs in psychology and education are typically developed from a privileged point of view and we don't even know it. And so, I very much appreciate the generosity of people who've paid a price for our work and our institutions, to help me reconfigure the constructs that we're talking about. So, when I talk about *diploma denial* now, rather than dropouts, I'm shifting the unit of analysis, right? I'm talking about policies that are denying young people diplomas rather than "Oh, you weren't very motivated," right? So, the project was participatory, insofar as we had a group of young people really helping us think about methods and questions and language, even though we fought a lot. . . . So, the participatory element really helped us understand the many ways these hyphens were playing in their lives.

The next step was to determine what kind of data to collect. Fine and Sirin first articulate the challenge of collecting data that would allow them to deeply explore the concept of hyphenated selves in contentious contexts (paragraph 10). After briefly describing the participants, the authors outline their approach to data collection, arguing for a mixed design that includes surveys, identity maps, and focus groups (paragraph 11). Specifically, they explain that their data needed to address two major needs. First, it needed to allow participants to describe themselves—to construct and articulate their identities—on and in their own terms. Paired with focus groups, the identity maps were designed to serve this purpose. Second, it needed to both create room for and describe intragroup variation, which was the primary rationale for collecting survey data. Again, this mandate was generated by the conceptual framework, which suggested that populations such as Muslim-American youth could not be easily reduced and categorized, and that understanding the experience of such populations thus needed to account for their heterogeneity.

The authors then describe, in detail, these data collection methods. They first turn to the use of identity maps, noting their methodological lineage and arguing for their suitability for this particular study (paragraphs 12 and 13). Of particular importance is the idea that these maps allow the participants to present or construct a social context around their sense of themselves; the instrument does not presuppose the nature of those relationships. "In the qualitative, we said: 'Draw your many selves,'" Fine explained. "We didn't structure it; we left it to them." Further, she explained, putting participants more in charge of the conversation opened up more opportunities for them to engage potentially sensitive topics, which in turn created a more fertile environment for the focus groups.

> [The identity maps] enabled young men and young women—particularly young men—to narrate affect that never would have come up either with focus group, or the surveys, or the individual interviews. . . . I just think it's a great method, because it legitimates the presence of politics, contradictions, and affect in identities and selves, in a way that asking people questions pulls for coherence. So, then they did these maps, and then, on the basis on that, they introduced themselves in the focus groups.

Fine and Sirin next describe how surveys were used to assess how the participants negotiated their identities as Muslim-American youth (paragraph 14), focusing on the role of survey data in differentiating the overarching concept of *Muslim-American* by allowing respondents to explain or define themselves as any combination of each, depending on specific domains or contexts. Here they had to walk a fine methodological line. On the one hand, they wanted to use the surveys to complicate either/or notions of identity. On the other hand, because it presupposes the importance of certain content and how questions should be asked, survey research tends to be less collaborative and participatory than other approaches to data collection. Fine described the challenge of thinking about traditional methods in unconventional ways:

> On the survey, I think we had a few different desires. One was not to set up any item where *Muslim* was at one end and *American* was at the other, to allow these strands of a braid to be narrated independently and interdependently, if they so chose, right? . . . And the young people helped us shape that. Now, so much of this literature says, you know, "Are you American, or are you Muslim?" Or "Are you Black, or are you American? Are you an immigrant?" Or, you know, "Do you live here or there?" And so this was a challenge, in the same way that transnationalism was a challenge. . . . So we're working against this dominant literature that's fixing and arguing opposition. So, I think I would say that we set up the survey to be able to interrogate each of those identities, and to what extent in the survey they overlap, so you can check *my friends,* or *my food,* or *my music,* or *both*. But also, statistically, to be able to say,

"These are unrelated." Which was a big, important finding. . . . But I was really glad to be able to pull those pieces out and say, this group of kids were all over the map, but these key, dominant notions are really operating in very, very different ways.

Finally, the authors explain the role of both maps and surveys in structuring and informing the focus groups (paragraph 15). These groups served two main purposes. First, they gave participants the opportunity to explicate and build upon their maps, with focus group facilitators prompting them about why they drew them the way they did. Second, as with all focus groups, it allowed these interpretations—descriptions of identity—to overlap and interact in a social setting, allowing participants to co-construct or further explain key themes together, and to articulate differences and similarities in their perceptions and experiences.

Fine and Sirin's use of identity maps combined—and strategically sequenced—with focus groups, surveys, and interviews speaks to the ways that they developed and implemented a research design that includes multiple, intersecting venues for the participants to share aspects of their identities and experiences in ways that can draw out their multilayered truths respectfully and with a particular attention and fidelity to the complexity of their social and psychological experiences as individuals and as a group living within a contentious sociopolitical milieu, one that changed on them in the middle of their adolescent identity development. This approach to data collection allows for more finely differentiated, complex data to emerge in a way that speaks to intragroup variation as a unit of analysis. It also has particular implications for data analysis. For one thing, the data collected for this study were deliberately not intended to "validate" one another. Instead, Fine and Sirin engineered into the study a certain tension, hoping that what they learned from and through each data source would allow them to make better sense of the others. Fine explained this tension as a different way of understanding triangulation as an analytic process, offering as an example the relationship between identity maps and survey data in the Muslim-American youth study.

I'm interested in what was called *triangulation*, but not to understand how different methods confirm each other, but the kind of jazz they create when you layer them on top of each other. You know, the kind of new music, not, "Oh yes, we're saying exactly the same thing in the surveys and the focus group." That just feels like a lack of imagination. But figuring out what this jazz is isn't always so easy. So, one of the ways we did that was to create these metacodes of the maps, and dividing them into *integrated*, *parallel*, and *conflicted*, and then laying those codes onto the survey data to see whether or not there were different dynamics. And certainly, in the conflicted ones, there were lots more reports of discrimination. . . . So, in some ways it became a way to validate the maps, but also to integrate qualitative and quantitative, or visual and statistical information.

For Fine and Sirin, the research is about keeping complexity vibrant and keeping explorations into Muslim-American youths' identities problematic, contested, and polyvocal. Fine and Sirin have chosen a conceptual framework and methodological approach that seek messiness rather than sterility; their research aims to understand the multilayered nature of the meanings the youth attribute to their identity descriptors in all of their range and variation rather than trying to flatten them out. Doing so requires not only a certain comfort level with ambiguity and complexity, but also a high degree of flexibility. The goal is not to develop a single, uniform "technique" for working across methods, but rather to remain systematic and transparent in how that work happens. In keeping with her relation of her topic to her stance as a researcher, Fine explained that this flexibility was needed to honor both the complexity of the topic and the views of the participants.

If you're going to mix methods, it's not to find sameness, but actually to work the complexity. So, I think the transport is an invitation to take these ideas to other contexts, but also to take with it the responsibility of its complexity . . . and not to turn it into a technique. . . . And so, I worry that transportability becomes standardization technique, and yet I also worry that people are diving into areas that are fragile and precious, and not very well protected, the way privileged spaces are protected, and that they feel free to say awful things. And so, it's a little bit of a call to responsibility, like I said. . . . So, maybe the hyphen's a way of, like, connecting those two as well, because method shouldn't be technique, but it should be systematic.

This statement about the responsibility of researchers to be reflexive is a call to action as much as it is a caveat and a validation of why to work with various identity groups, especially when their experience is shaped by being systematically marginalized and is ideally a recursive process of critical, iterative conceptual and methodological development. These caveats are borne from Fine's experience engaging in research into delicate, complex topics with populations that have often been marginalized and mistreated in ways that affect her research. Fine's statement about looking for complexity, of having a responsibility to be ideologically loyal and methodologically attentive to complexity, is at the core of her decades-long research career. Her resistance to viewing methods as technique, while arguing that they should be rigorous and systematic, is at the center of debates in the field of qualitative research in particular, debates about how one achieves methodological rigor while at the same time resisting theoretical and methodological rigidity. This is a delicate balance, but, as we see in works like "Theorizing Hyphenated Selves," achieving this kind of fidelity to complex theoretical and methodological approaches is possible as long as conceptual-methodological choices are intentional and transparent and become, themselves, a domain for critical inquiry.

## ☆ CONCEPTUAL FRAMEWORKS AND FIELDWORK: CONCLUDING THOUGHTS

We conclude this chapter with a statement about the nature of conceptual frameworks and their influence on data collection and fieldwork choices. As has been shown in this chapter, conceptual frameworks are simultaneously guides for and products of an iterative, ever-evolving process of development that happens through dialogic and internal processes of meaning making on the part of the researcher, processes that challenge and refute as well as support and uphold specific theoretical and ideological influences on the research. We argue that it is precisely through reckoning with the tensions and crosscurrents that arise when one scrutinizes the influences on their research that the most creative, elucidating research findings emerge (Jaffee, Kling, Plant, Sloan, & Hyde, 1999; Russell & Bohan, 1999).

Michelle Fine's work offers an excellent example of the close relationship between who you are, what you study, and how you study it. A conceptual framework is actually the embodiment of all three. As a researcher, you make choices about what you think is important or interesting; those choices are reflections of who you are as a person. They are also reflections of where and with whom you work. The language you use to describe the research, the methods you employ, and how you write up and present results are all a function of the social, political, and professional worlds you inhabit as a scholar. By highlighting Fine's work, we hope to make explicit the nature of this relationship.

More generally, this chapter illustrates how conceptual frameworks inform methodology. Simply put, the ways in which you argue for a particular topic or focus profoundly influence the range of methodological options available to you. Fine's own interest in breaking through fixed (and in her view, pejorative) conceptions of "other," or non-American, identity necessitated a different approach to survey design and a more open, participatory form of qualitative data collection. The choices you make about what data you collect are in turn intimately tied to how you are able to analyze those data. It is to this aspect of methodology that we turn in the next chapter.

## READING REFERENCES ☆

Abu El-Haj, T. R. (2005). Global politics, dissent, and Palestinian American identities: Engaging conflict to reinvigorate democratic education. In L. Weis & M. Fine (Eds.), *Beyond silenced voices: Class, race, and gender in U.S. Schools* (rev. ed., pp. 199–216). Albany State University of New York Press.

Appadurai, A. (2004). The capacity to aspire. In V. Rao & M. Walton (Eds.), *Culture and public action* (pp. 59–85). Stanford, CA: Stanford University Press.

Berry, J. W. (1997). Immigration, acculturation, and adaptation. *Applied Psychology: An International Review, 46,* 5–68.

Berry, J. W., & Kim, U. (1988). Acculturation and mental health. In P. R. Dasen, J. W. Berry, & N. Satorius (Eds.), *Health and cross-cultural psychology: Towards applications, cross cultural research and methodology series.* (Vol. 10, pp. 207–236). Thousand Oaks, CA: Sage.

Bhabha, H. (2005). "Race," time and the revision of modernity. In C. McCarthy, W. Crichlow, G. Dimitriadis, & N. Dolby (Eds.), *Race, identity, and representation in education* (pp. 13–26). New York: Routledge.

Cainkar, L. (2004). The impact of the September 11 attacks and their aftermath on Arab and Muslim communities in the United States. *Global Security Quarterly, 13.*

Deaux, K., & Philogone, G. (Eds.). (2001). *Representations of the social: Bridging theoretical traditions.* Oxford, UK: Breakwell.

Erikson, E. (1980). *Identity and the life cycle.* New York: Norton. (Original work published 1959)

Fine, M. (1991). *Framing dropouts: Notes on the politics of an urban public high school.* Albany: State University of New York Press.

Fine, M., Burns, A., Payne, Y., & Torre, M. E. (2004). Civics lessons: The color and class of betrayal. *Teachers College Record, 106,* 2193–2223.

Fine, M., Roberts, R. A., Torre, M. E., Bloom, J., Burns, A., Chajet, L., et al. (2004). *Echoes of Brown: Youth documenting and performing the legacy of* Brown v. Board of Education. New York: Teachers College Press.

Fine, M., & Torre, M. E. (2004). Re-membering exclusions: Participatory action research in public institutions. *Qualitative Research in Psychology, 1*(1), 15–37.

Fisher, C. B., Wallace, S. A., & Fenton, R. E. (2000). Discrimination distress during adolescence. *Journal of Youth and Adolescence, 29,* 679–695.

Geiseking, J. (2007). *A brief summary of mental mapping.* Unpublished manuscript, City University of New York.

Gerges, F. A. (2003). Islam and Muslims in the mind of America. *Annals of the American Academy of Political and Social Science, 588*, 73–89.

Hart, R. A. (1981). Children's spatial representations of the landscape: Lessons and questions from a field study. In L. S. Liben, A. H. Patterson, & N. Newcombe (Eds.), *Spatial representation and behavior across the life span* (pp. 195–233). San Diego, CA: Academic Press.

Harvey, D. (2001). Capitalism: The factory of fragmentation. In *Spaces of capital* (pp. 121–127). New York: Routledge.

Helms, J. E. (Ed.). (1990). *Black and white racial identity: Theory, research, and practice*. New York: Greenwood.

Katz, C. (2003). *Growing up global*. Minneapolis: University of Minnesota Press.

LaFromboise, T., Coleman, H. L. K., & Gerton, J. (1993). Psychological impact of biculturalism: Evidence and theory. *Psychological Bulletin, 114*, 395–412.

Levitt, P. (2000). Migrants participate across borders: Toward an understanding of forms and consequences. In N. Foner, R. Rumbaut, & S. Gold (Eds.), *Immigration research for a new century* (pp. 459–480). New York: Russell Sage Foundation.

Lorenzo, M. K., Frost, A. K., & Reinherz, H. Z. (2000). Social and emotional functioning of older Asian American adolescents. *Child and Adolescent Social Work Journal, 17*, 289–304.

Luhtanen, R., & Crocker, J. (1992). A collective self-esteem scale: Self evaluation of one's social identity. *Personality and Social Psychology Bulletin, 18*, 302–318.

Lynch, K. (1960). *The image of the city*. Cambridge: MIT Press.

Milgram, S., & Jodelet, D. (1976). Psychological maps of Paris. In H. Proshansky, W. Ittelson, & L. Rivlin (Eds.), *Environmental psychology* (pp. 104–124). New York: Holt, Rinehart and Winston.

Nesdale, D., Rooney, R., & Smith, L. (1997). Migrant ethnic identity and psychological distress. *Journal of Cross-Cultural Psychology, 28*, 569–588.

Oppedal, B., Røysamb, E., & Heyerdahl, S. (2005). Ethnic group, acculturation, and psychiatric problems in young immigrants. *Journal of Child Psychology and Psychiatry, 46*, 646–660.

Oppedal, B., Roysamb, E., & Sam, D. L. (2004). The effect of acculturation and social support on change in mental health among young immigrants. *International Journal of Behavioral Development, 28*, 481–494.

Phinney, J. S., Cantu, C., & Kurtz, D. A. (1997). Ethnic and American identity as predictors of self-esteem among African American, Latino, and White adolescents. *Journal of Youth and Adolescence, 26*(2), 165–185.

Rao, V., & Walton, M. (2004). *Culture and public action*. Stanford, CA: Stanford University Press.

Rizvi, F. (2005). Representations of Islam and education for justice. In C. McCarthy, W. Crichlow, G. Dimitriadis, & N. Dolby (Eds.), *Race, identity, and representation in education* (pp. 167–178). New York: Routledge.

Romero, A. J., & Roberts, R. E. (2003). Stress within a bicultural context for adolescents of Mexican descent. *Cultural Diversity & Ethnic Minority Psychology, 9*(2), 171–184.

Saarinen, T. F. (1973). Student views of the world. In R. M. Downs & D. Stea (Eds.), *Image and environment: Cognitive mapping and spatial behavior* (pp. 148–161). Chicago: Aldine.

Sen, A. (2004). How does culture matter? In V. Rao & M.Walton (Eds.), *Culture and public action* (pp. 37–58). Stanford, CA: Stanford University Press.

Shohat, E. (2006). *Taboo memories, diasporic voices.* Durham, NC: Duke University Press.

Sirin, S. R., Diemmer, M. A., Jackson, L. R., Gonsalves, L., & Howell, A. (2004). Future aspirations of urban adolescents: A person-in-context model. *International Journal of Qualitative Studies in Education, 17,* 437–459.

Sirin, S. R., & Rogers-Sirin, L. (2005). Components of school engagement among African American adolescents. *Applied Developmental Science, 9*(1), 5–13.

Solis, J. (2003). Rethinking illegality as violence against, not by, Mexican immigrant children and youth. *Journal of Social Issues, 59*(1), 15–32.

Suarez-Orozco, C. (2005). Identities under siege: Immigration stress and social mirroring among the children of immigrants. In A. Robben & M. Suarez-Orozco (Eds.), *Cultures under siege: Social violence and trauma* (pp. 194–226). Cambridge, UK: Cambridge University Press.

Way, N., & Robinson, M. (2003). The influence of family and friends on the psychological adjustment of ethnic minority, low-income adolescents. *Journal of Adolescent Research, 18,* 324–347.

Wilkinson, S. (1999). Focus groups: A feminist method. *Psychology of Women Quarterly, 23,* 221–244.

Wilkinson, S., & Kitzinger, C. (Eds.). (1995). *Representing the other.* London: Sage.

Wilkinson, S., & Kitzinger, C. (2000). Thinking differently about thinking positive: A discursive approach to cancer patients' talk. *Social Science & Medicine, 50,* 797–811.

Wilkinson, S., & Kitzinger, C. (2003). Constructing identities: A feminist conversation analytic approach to positioning in action. In R. Harre & F. Moghaddam (Eds.), *The self and others: Positioning individuals and groups in personal, political and cultural contexts* (pp. 157–180). New York: Praeger/Greenwood.

Willis, P. (2002). Foot soldiers of modernity: The dialectics of cultural consumption and the 21st century school. In C. McCarthy, W. Crichlow, G. Dimitriadis, & N. Dolby (Eds.), *Race, identity, and representation in education* (pp. 461–479). New York: Routledge.

Winnicott, D. W., Winnicott, C., Shepard, R., & Davis, M. (Eds.). (1989). *Psychoanalytic explorations: D.W. Winnicott.* Cambridge, MA: Harvard University Press.

Yuval-Davis, N. (2001). *The binary war.* Retrieved from http://www.opendemocracy .net/conflict-war_on_terror/article_89.jsp

# CHAPTER 5

# CONCEPTUAL FRAMEWORKS AND THE ANALYSIS OF DATA

Just as data collection is a series of decisions about how a researcher interacts with the setting, data analysis is a series of choices about how you interact with the data. We argue in this book that a conceptual framework offers a clear, consistent frame of reference for making methodological decisions, including choices about how you organize, interpret, and, ultimately, analyze (and as we will see in this chapter, reanalyze) data. This chapter moves us from explicating the role of conceptual frameworks in designing and collecting data in empirical studies to what you *do* with those data once you have collected them: how you conceptualize data, frame data theoretically, how you develop arguments based on what you see in and discern from your data sets. At its ideal, a conceptual framework informs data analysis in direct, meaningful, transparent ways. It helps you decide what is most important to emphasize or focus on, provides you with tools for organizing and filtering the data, and helps you make choices about where and when to work inductively or deductively. It also justifies and makes visible your own interpretive processes, which (as we detailed in the previous chapter) are themselves shaped by your intellectual, ideological, or political commitments.

## ☆ EXAMINING THE INFLUENCE OF AN EVER-EMERGING CONCEPTUAL FRAMEWORK

To illustrate this process, we analyze "Going for the Zone: The Social and Cognitive Ecology of Teacher-Student Interaction in Classroom Conversations," written by Frederick Erickson. Erickson is an educational anthropologist who has helped shape the field of qualitative research and has been a methodological innovator throughout his career. We explore Erickson's process of data analysis to explicate the interpretive process as a series of decisions about how a researcher interacts with the data and how this is guided by conceptual leanings as it informs them. We use this analysis of Erickson's methodological choices to explain how conceptual frameworks inform a researcher's process of choice-making and framing. We specifically examine how conceptual frameworks inform analytic themes (and vice versa) and discuss the role of various modes of data analysis, including transcription, data organization, and theory building, in relation to what we think of as the inductive-deductive continuum.

"Going for the Zone" is based on Erickson's research in a kindergarten and first-grade classroom. After discussing background and context for the chapter, we move into an examination of the text as a means to understand how a researcher's conceptual framework both directly and indirectly informs his analytical choices and methods. While these aspects of the research process are typically talked about in isolation, we seek to relate them in ways that do justice to the important role a conceptual framework plays in the analytic process. We chose to include this piece of Erickson's research for several reasons. First, his work in general, and this article in particular, occurs at the intersection of multiple fields, and thus integrates ways of thinking about and doing research from different perspectives. Second, for the better part of his career he has been an innovator in data analysis—something that is readily apparent in this article. Finally, he has analyzed this specific data set using a range of theories, allowing us to see the implications of his conceptual framework for his findings and the arguments he arrives at in "Going for the Zone."

## ☆ ABOUT THE AUTHOR

Frederick Erickson is George F. Kneller Professor of Anthropology of Education and Professor of Applied Linguistics at the University of California, Los Angeles (UCLA). Originally trained in music, with an undergraduate and master's degree in music composition and music history, he became engaged in volunteer music teaching in an inner-city YMCA in Chicago, where he later did youth work and participated in the civil rights movement as a volunteer in the Southern Christian Leadership Conference's northern urban initiative. He earned his PhD in education at Northwestern University in 1969. Since then he has taught at the University of Illinois-Chicago, Harvard University, Michigan State University, and the University of Pennsylvania. His contributions to the field of anthropology of education have earned him numerous honors and awards, including fellowships from the Spencer Foundation and the Annenberg Institute for Public Policy, a Fulbright award, the Spindler Award for Scholarly Contributions to Educational Anthropology from the American Anthropological Association, and a Lifetime Achievement Award for Research on the Social Context of Education from Division G of the American Educational Research Association (AERA). Erickson's writings on the video-based microethnographic study of classroom and family interaction and on qualitative research methods more generally are widely cited. His recent book, *Talk and Social Theory: Ecologies of Speaking and Listening in Everyday Life* (Polity Press, 2004), received an Outstanding Book Award for 2005 from AERA. He serves on the editorial boards of *Research on Language and Social Interaction*, *Discourse and Communication*, *International Review of Qualitative Research*, and *Teachers College Record*. In 1998–1999 and again in 2006–2007 he was a fellow at the Center for Advanced Study in the Behavioral Sciences at Stanford University. In 2000 he was elected a member of the National Academy of Education, and in 2009 he was elected a fellow of AERA.

## BACKGROUND AND CONTEXT: AN ☆ OVERVIEW OF THE WORK IN FOCUS

Human interaction is not rocket science. It's far more complicated than that. Language alone, with its multiple formal and informal meanings, is astonishingly complex. But interaction is much more than language. Nonverbal communication, often subtle, can change the meaning of words; changes in tone (in the case of sarcasm, for instance) indicate meanings that are qualitatively different from the literal definition of a word. Speakers are governed by unwritten rules about interruption and turn-taking, which can be bent or broken with the assistance of verbal and nonverbal cues, and different styles of speaking may be considered appropriate or inappropriate depending on the setting and context, the speaker, or the listener.

For the most part, we humans are remarkably adept at negotiating this complexity. But as globalization brings about ever more intercultural contact, the instances of disjuncture—moments when the people interacting are governed by different sets of rules—become ever more common. All of which lends added importance to a question that we take for granted in our everyday lives: how does interaction work?

For decades, anthropologists and sociolinguists have grappled with this fundamental question. In education, they have focused on the added dimension of what happens when certain ways of interacting are considered "normal" or acceptable while others are not. Understanding the broad spheres of influence on everyday encounters in educational spaces such as schools and classrooms, for example, has helped educational theorists, researchers, and practitioners—and those of us who inhabit multiple roles—to engage critically, in contextualized ways, in analyses of school- and classroom-based conditions, realities, and relationships. In this vein, Frederick Erickson's research has contributed a great deal to our understanding of relational dynamics and their educational implications in terms of how these are framed and shaped by larger sociopolitical circumstances that instantiate themselves in seemingly small microinteractions.

Like much of Erickson's work, "Going for the Zone" resides at the intersection of theories about interaction, culture, and learning—an intellectual space that was created in part through the work of cultural psychologist Lev Vygotsky. Though criticized during and after his own lifetime, Vygotsky's work enjoyed a renaissance in the second half of the twentieth century. Among scholars, his work fit comfortably with evolving theories of distributed cognition and situated learning (Cole & Engestrom, 1993; Lave & Wenger, 1991), while pedagogical trends (back) toward cooperative learning and constructivism buoyed its status among educational practitioners. A full discussion of Vygotsky's work is not needed here. Suffice it to say that these intellectual and educational trends signaled a shift from thinking about learning as something that happens inside people's heads (a view generally, if oversimplistically, ascribed to Piaget) to something that happens in the interactions among them. In the academic world, this shift brought fields and disciplines that had previously been more distant or even opposed into close contact. Those who studied cognition and those who studied interaction found themselves on common ground (if not necessarily in agreement) in conversations about the nature of learning.

During this time, Frederick Erickson was part of a group that was working to redefine and extend our understanding of how interaction works. As he began his doctoral research at Northwestern University, Erickson was influenced by early work in sociolinguistics and ethnography of communication, along with psychological research on nonverbal behavior and communication. These lines of research converged on a view of conversation and interaction that was ecological in nature. In our interview with him about his empirical work, Erickson explained:

The idea was there is this ecology of mutual influence between everybody who is a participant in the scene, and you didn't just focus on the lead speaker. You were looking at the whole thing in a kind of ecosystem perspective.

This in turn gave rise to a more nuanced understanding of the context in (and with) which communication occurred. By the 1970s, context was no longer seen as the backdrop to interaction, but something that was created through interaction itself. Erickson explained the significance of this development:

In Ray McDermott's doctoral thesis, there's this wonderful line where he says, "People in interaction," I think maybe he said, "constitute contexts for one another." So, context isn't outside the text of the interaction; it's in it, as well as outside it. So, that was another, kind of fundamental assumption we were using. . . . If you don't realize that within a given event there may be many different phases, each with a different participation structure, each a new context, you're going to do things that were appropriate in the previous one, but that aren't now.

It was around this time that what Erickson terms "neo-Vygotskian" perspectives began to enter the literature. Among those who studied interaction, this was a welcome development. But Erickson and his colleagues found the neo-Vygotskian perspective on interaction to be simplistic, and perhaps a bit naïve. "This notion of interaction in the zone of proximal development (ZPD) seemed curiously sociologically innocent," he recalled.

The early writing about engagement [in the ZPD] . . . made it seem as if that engagement itself was unproblematic, right? And all you had to do was just get two people together, and they would form this ZPD, and then everything would be just smooth sailing from then on. And by then I had been in a whole bunch of classrooms . . . and I was more and more persuaded that simply establishing something like a relationship in the zone of proximal development was interactionally so much more complicated than people were thinking about.

The material that eventually became "Going for the Zone" was originally developed for a lecture Erickson was asked to give by a colleague. By this point, he had for some time been studying the fine-grained structures and processes underlying communication in classrooms, and had developed some innovative approaches to doing so. The idea of critiquing the neo-Vygotskian view occurred to him as he thought about how to frame and introduce this way of studying communication to a new audience.

The kind of invocation of Vygotsky was the new thing that I added, given that I was going to be talking to these people who knew about that. . . . Thinking that this is a rhetorically effective way to make the point that interaction itself is the learning environment, and it's a whole lot more complicated than the way most people talk about it.

Framing his work along new theoretical lines was far more than just rhetorical sleight of hand, however. For the argument to be persuasive, Erickson had to show not only that the critique had theoretical merit, but that the data he presented and the way he analyzed it would support that critique. In the excerpt and discussion that follow, we show how he approached this and, in the process, highlight the tight relationship between conceptual framework and the framing and analysis of data.

There were many twists and turns in the road to making the argument presented in "Going for the Zone." Some of these twists were caused by shifts within and across generations of thinkers and how those germinated across fields and instantiated themselves in his point of view at the time of writing the chapter. This historical moment within and across fields directly framed Erickson's thinking as well as how he envisioned his audience and therefore constructed the messages he wished to communicate. This process of deciding how to enter into a conversation already happening requires the intentional making of interpretive choices about how to enter these discussions conceptually.

> Erickson, F. (1996). Going for the zone: The social and cognitive ecology of teacher-student interaction in classroom conversations. In D. Hicks (Ed.), *Discourse, learning, and schooling* (pp. 29–62). Cambridge, UK: Cambridge University Press; Reprinted with the permission of Cambridge University Press.

## Social interaction as a learning environment

[1] Research and theory construction along neo-Vygotskian lines has presented cognition in a new light: as socially situated (a kind of production that makes purposive use of tools, including those others have made) and as transpersonal (a distributed phenomenon, not simply something residing within a single head). This makes for a profound change in how we think about thinking, about learning, and about teaching—participation by teachers and pupils in nonverbal interaction and in oral and written conversation—the interaction among people that fosters learning.

[2] How does the mutual influence we call teaching and learning actually take place in and through immediate social interaction? Neo-Vygotskian

work has emphasized the importance of social interaction in learning. It points to the engagement of expert and novice in the zone of proximal development (ZPD), through which the more expert party in the interchange helps to complete and extend the actions and insights of the less expert one.

[3] Yet, if social interaction is seen as crucial for learning, we must not leave unexamined the notion of social interaction itself. My sense is that in much of the neo-Vygotskian work, what has occupied the foreground of attention is the cognitive or linguistic changes that occur in the learner rather than the processes of interaction through which such changes are seen as being stimulated. Analyses of transcripts of expert-novice dialogue focus on the content of speech rather than on the process of interaction in tandem with its manifest content. In other words, interaction as a social and behavioral process seems to be treated as a residual category in discussions of engagement in the ZPD. Thus it is possible that unexamined assumptions about the nature of social interaction (and of conversation) as a medium for learning and teaching may be constraining the ways in which pedagogical transactions are being viewed.

## Conceptions of social interaction

[4] Neo-Vygotskian discussions of engagement in the ZPD place special emphasis on two aspects of social interaction—the dyadic and the reciprocal. Perhaps because of the origins of the notion of ZPD in the interactive experiments of Vygotsky, the learning situation is seen as one involving a single expert and a single novice (see, e.g., Vygotsky 1978; Wertsch 1985; Wood, Bruner, & Ross 1976).

[5] Dialogue is a powerful and evocative metaphor for the transformative engagement that happens in conversation. Yet the organization of talk in classrooms is not literally dialogic, that is, classrooms are not just settings for verbal exchanges between pairs of individuals in isolation from others around them. That view comes in part from idealized images of pedagogical conversations such as that of Mark Hopkins and a student sitting on either end of a log, or of the teacher-student dialogues from classical, medieval, and renaissance educational texts (which themselves probably derive from Plato's idealized presentation of Socrates in dialogue with one primary interlocutor at a time). Prescriptive models of "good teaching" often treat classroom conversation as if it were a series of one-on-one engagements

between the teacher and a succession of students. Classroom etiquette for recitation (nowadays considered an aspect of classroom management) and the ubiquity in whole-class discussion of what many researchers call the *IRE* discourse sequence (known information question initiated by the teacher, followed by a response by a student, followed in turn by evaluation of the response by the teacher) may imply a cultural model of "one speaker at a time and pairs of speakers in dialogue" for the social participation framework of ordinary classroom conversation.

[6] In my experience, much classroom interaction is far messier than this, even when children are being nice. Children stumble over each other in conversation. They may complete each other's clauses and turns at talk. They may take turns away from each other. The pullings and counterpullings, the ebbs and flows of mutual influence in the conversation, are not just between one student and the teacher at a given time but rather among many students—sometimes among teams of students—and the teacher. How, then, does a single student get to a ZPD with a teacher? And need the single student get there alone or can multiple students enter a ZPD together? Do we mean only dyadic engagement when we conceive of interaction in the ZPD?

[7] The other notion about interaction implicit in the neo-Vygotskian work is that it is reciprocal in a sequential sense; that is, one party's action is seen as being followed by another's in response across successive moments in real time. From this point of view (the usual one), human social interaction is conceived as a ping-pong match. Successful participation by speakers, and the influence of one speaker on another, are seen as involving syntagmatically appropriate matchings of one person's initiation with another person's response across successive moments in real time (e.g., if person X asks a question, then person Y is accountable for answering it at the next appropriate moment).

[8] Yet this emphasis on sequential reciprocity (which centers our attention on turntaking in oral discourse) overlooks the complementarity of simultaneous participation in interaction by interlocutors. More than turntaking is going on. At the same moments in which the speaker is speaking, the listener is listening. Because the speaker can see as well as hear, whatever the listener is doing nonverbally (and verbally) is available as evidence that what the speaker is saying is being received by the auditor.

[9] Given the complexity of reciprocal and complementary organization that is necessary to accomplish a multiparty conversation successfully, we must ask, "How does the sociocognitive ecology work in classroom conversations? How is the collective action done so that interactional (and cognitive) traffic jams do not occur and so that there is an opportunity for understanding and learning?" In attempting to answer such questions, we may come to see how insights gained from analysis of the workings of interactional traffic management in classroom conversations can inform a theory of cognition and learning as situated, collective, and purposive human activity. (pp. 32–34)

## Traffic management in interaction: Timing and contextualization cues

[10] Timing appears to be what holds the whole ecology of interaction together in its performance. The relative temporal location of the various actions of interlocutors is an important aspect of the ordering of the collective activity of conversation in both its reciprocal and its complementary aspects. We can speak of timing as one aspect of a dialectical process in interaction that has been called contextualization by Gumperz (1982; see also Erickson, 1992), entailing a system of signals he calls contextualization cues. The notion of contextualization follows that of Bateson (1956), who observed that because of an inherent ambiguity in systems of communicative signs, those engaged in interaction need to regulate it by signals that point to the relevant context of interpretation in which other signs are intended to be "read." Thus sets of communicative displays contain, within the surface structure of their performance, certain behavioral features that function as cues that point to their proper interpretation. In other words, the enactment of communication reflexively creates its contextual framing at the same time as it is being framed by its context.

[11] In the timing of immediate social interaction, such as in face-to-face conversation, an especially important contextualizing function appears to be performed by the temporal placement of points of emphasis in speech prosody (volume and pitch shifts) and in body motion (postural shifts, gaze, changes in direction of motion in gesture). The points of emphasis appear to function as contextualization cues that signal expectations at various levels. Not only do individual cues of

verbal or nonverbal emphasis enable one to anticipate immediate next moments, but because they tend to cluster together in regular intervals of occurrence, the clusters of points of emphasis in speech and body motion often can be perceived as a cadence. This cadence is a rhythmic underpinning that enables the various participants in a conversational interchange to anticipate the projected courses of action of individual interlocutors and of the conversational group as a whole (see the discussion in Erickson, 1992).

[12] This sense of "rightness" of time is pointed to by a distinction in Greek between time in a technical or physical sense and in a social and phenomenological sense. The former conception of time is meant by the term *chronos*, from which we derive terms for clock time and for the quantitatively uniform measurement of units of time. The latter understanding is meant by the term *kairos*, which refers to the developing or unfolding quality of time: change of seasons, of weather, of crucial turning points in history. This is time as humanly experienced: "in the fullness of time"; the emergent "not quite yet"; the "now" that, once arrived, feels right.

[13] In human social interaction, *kairos* timing results from the mutual activity of the interactional partners. It is not absolutely regular chronometrically; there is an ebb and flow of speeding up and slowing down that in music is called rubato. Yet conversational partners share a mutually enacted timing that is remarkably predictable. At some moments, it is almost chronometric, but not quite. At other times, rhythmic stress in speech and in body motion (i.e., posture, gesture, and gaze) is virtually metronomic in its chronometric regularity. At this point, the significance of *kairos* timing for the organization of interaction is only beginning to be realized (see the discussion in Auer, 1992; Cooper-Kuhlen, 1992; Erickson, 1982, 1992; Erickson & Shultz, 1982, 72–74; Scollon, 1982).

[14] In sum, we can say that timing enables nothing less than the social organization of attention and action in conversation. Moreover, we can say that the timing of interactional performance is accomplished by contextualization cuing. Hence when we say that cognition and action are situated in sociocognitive learning environments, we mean, among other things, that they are situated in real time—not an ideal "time-out" condition for reflection and deliberation but an actual, ongoing development of sequences of interaction, moment by moment, in which one is never completely sure of where the interaction is going next and during which the time clock never stops.

[15] At (28) Miss Wright turned further to her left to look at the chalk-board behind her. Now she asked another question, and it was a known-information one: "You remember what the name of that let-ter is?" She paused and Angie did not answer. "[The letter] that looks like a snake?" she prompted, tracing the sinuous letter with her hand. Angie still did not answer. "What . . ." Miss Walsh began with another prompt.

[16] In the silence of the turn allocated to Angie, three other students answered at (29–31): "S! . . S . . . S . . ." Miss Wright looked away from Angie and around to her right at the speakers, shaking her head. "No," and saying "Sh . . . You're right but let's let Angie tell it." The turn sharks had struck again.

(23) T:    (*looks back to L*)

    What else do you like about school?

(24) A:    <u>Play</u>. . . .

(25) T:    What do you like to do best in school?

(26) A:    Play <u>blocks</u> . . .

(27) T:    Play with <u>blocks</u> . . is that your favorite thing? . .

(28) T:    (*turns to her left, then points left hand to chalkboard behind her*)

    You remember what the name of that

    <u>letter</u> is . . (*Angie does not speak*)  that looks like a

    <u>snake</u>? . . (*Angie does not speak* )

    <u>What</u> . . . (*Angie does not speak*)

(29) S-1:   S . .

(30) S-2:   S . .

(31) S-3:   S . .

(32) T:    (*looks around to her right at speakers, shakes head, "No," . . and smiles*)

    Sh . . You're

    <u>right</u> but let's let

    <u>Angie</u> tell it . .

[17] Notice (at 28–31), the time at which Angie did not speak and the other students did. At (28) the teacher asked Angie, "You remember what the name of that letter is?" The pause after that question was

the *kairos* time in which an answer was appropriate. But Angie did not answer then, nor did she do so after a prompt by the teacher that was followed by another prompt, ". . . that looks like a snake? . . . What/." Finally, three other students said the answer, *"S."*

[18] Someone needed to answer, and do so in the right time. But not just anyone. As indicated by the prior verbal exchanges with the teacher and by the teacher's nonverbal signals of posture and gaze orientation, it was Angie who had been designated by the teacher as the appropriate utterer of the answer that was summoned by the question. The teacher had been looking at Angie. When she looked away to her left (at 28), she did not look at another student, which might have been taken as an implicit cue nominating someone other than Angie as the next designated speaker. (Often the teacher signaled that one child's air time was over and another's was beginning by looking away from the prior speaker to another student whose air time would be next.) But in this case, in looking away from Angie, the teacher looked at the chalkboard. Thus, even though gaze and full frontal postural orientation with Angie were broken by the teacher, her glance to the board can be taken as maintaining rather than changing Angie's right to the floor. Angie was still being framed by the teacher's cues as the designated next speaker—the person who should answer the question just asked, and who should do so in the next moment of the discourse.

[19] How do we know it is a *next* moment? How did the teacher, Angie, and the other students know when that "next" moment had arrived? We can infer that their inferences about the *when* of the answer slot have to do with the *kairos* timing cues discussed earlier. A succession of stressed syllables of speech mark a cadence together with markers of kinesic prominence, such as change in the direction of motion in a gesture, with shifts in postural position, and with shifts in gaze direction. Prior time intervals in that cadence could be taken as if they marked a metronome beat. Thus a succession of rhythmic, regularly spaced beats on prior moments enabled one, in the current moment of a "now" beat, to estimate how long it would be until the "next" beat would occur. Interactants could thus hold an expectation of the actual occurrence at a "next" and "go for" it, reaching for it by speech or gesture that projects a trajectory that will be completed on the cadence point of the next beat.

[20] The following transcription (Figure 5.1), using musical notation, shows how the next moment for the answer "S" was being projected

in Angie's and the teacher's interactional behavior. The transcription begins with the question by the teacher at (23), "What else do you like about school?"

[21] Notice that in measure (2) there were two stressed syllables in the teacher's speech, "else" and "school." In measure (3), after a pause of exactly the same duration as the interval between "else" and "two" in the previous measure, Angie said "Play," thus answering the teacher's question. Notice a similar pattern in measure (5), where the pause after the stressed word "best" in the teacher's question "What do you like to do *best* in school?" Angie said, "Play *blocks.*" In this case the word "play" was unstressed—said as a "pickup note" to the stressed word that followed, *"blocks."* That stressed word came at the same time interval as that between the previous stressed word, *"best,"* and the pause in the teacher's speech that followed. From this it would seem that the appropriate time for an answer to be uttered to a question by the teacher is either the next "beat" after the end of the teacher's question or the next "beat" after that. If the cadence established across stressed syllables or words is approximately 1 second, then the student has 1 second, or at most 2 seconds, to respond to the teacher's question. After 1 or 2 seconds, either the teacher will prompt the designated answerer (often beginning the prompt on the next beat after the silence by the student) or another student will attempt to answer.

[22] In these cases, the questions asked for information that Angie alone knew, and she answered them with a stressed word uttered on the "beat" immediately after the end of the teacher's question. This left no room either for a prompt by the teacher or for an attempt by another student to take away the answer turn by filling the rhythmically cued answer slot with an answer of his or her own.

[23] Then the teacher revoiced Angie's utterance, "Play *blocks,*" with a slight syntactic expansion, "Play with the *blocks.*" (Notice that in making this slight paraphrase, a shift to a more formally elaborated style by including the conjunction and definite article, the teacher echoed the rhythmic placement of Angie's utterance; in the teacher's utterance, primary stress still fell on "blocks," with the previous syllables uttered as a triplet of "upbeats" preparing for the stressed word, "blocks.") At measure (8) the teacher began to ask another question: "You remember what the name of that letter is?" Unlike the previous questions, this was a teacherlike known-information question. As the teacher uttered the question, she turned and pointed to the board.

**Figure 5.1**  Rhythmic organization of questions and answers about school and letter name

[24] Angie's eyes followed the sweep of the teacher's arm as Angie directed her gaze to the chalkboard where the teacher was pointing. But notice the first beat of measure (9)—the beat immediately after the end of the teacher's question. Unlike the two previous occasions when Angie had answered on the next beat after the last stressed syllable in the question

(measures 2–3 and 5–6), this time on the next beat after the teacher's question Angie did not answer. In measure (9) the teacher responded to Angie's silence with a prompt, ". . . that looks like a *snake?*" Still no answer. On the next beat the teacher started another prompt: "what." As she said this, one other child answered "S" just after the beat. On the next beat, the second beat of measure (10), another child answered. Finally, on the next beat (measure 11), the teacher, who had by then looked away from Angie to the other speakers, addressed them by saying, "You're *right,*" and went on to say, "but let's let *Angie* tell it." As the teacher said "you're *right,*" she placed the stressed word on the immediately next beat, just as had Angie and the other children when they were filling answer slots after the teacher's questions. Thus the teacher's utterance, "you're *right,*" on the second beat of measure (11) can be heard as an "answer" to the students' saying "S" in answering the question that had originally been directed at Angie.

# THE ARGUMENT ☆

The argument at the center of "Going for the Zone" is about how we understand interaction. Erickson builds from the general idea that cognition is social and interactive to a more specific point about the nature of that interaction. This in turn establishes the rationale for a close analysis of the timing of interaction. The overarching argument can be summarized as follows:

1. Neo-Vygotskian thinking reflects a shift toward viewing cognition as socially situated and interactive, and therefore constitutes a fundamental change in how learning and thinking are viewed (paragraphs 1 and 2).

2. However, if we are to locate interaction at the center of thinking and learning, it is important to pay close attention to the nature of interaction itself. To really understand how the ZPD functions, we need to know something about how conversation works, and this is no simple matter (paragraphs 3 and 4). Specifically, we need to account for two important aspects of interaction.

3. First, it does not tend to occur in the form of orderly dialogue (paragraphs 5 and 6).

4. Second, it is considerably more complicated than a sequence of turns taken by the various speakers. In addition to what is being

said at any given moment, listening, feedback, and nonverbal communication all shape the interaction (paragraphs 7 and 8). This complexity must be negotiated and managed in order to avoid cognitive and conversational "traffic jams," and thus provide opportunities for learning.

5. This is primarily achieved through timing (paragraph 10), which refers both to the temporal sequence of utterances and other communicative behaviors, *chronos*, but also to the successful identification of "right" or appropriate instances for those behaviors within the stream of the interaction, *kairos* (paragraph 12).

6. This timing is determined not only by what is said, but by all of the other contextual and nonverbal cues that people use to figure out the timing of conversation (paragraphs 11 and 13).

7. To truly understand, therefore, how a ZPD is established (or not established) within classroom interactions, it is necessary to explore the timing of those interactions (paragraph 14).

At the heart of "Going for the Zone" are numerous pages (approximately 9 out of 31) of deep, focused, and specific line-by-line analysis in which Erickson uses data to ground his interpretations and theorize interaction. He accomplishes this through the use of a multilayered analytical approach in "an attempt to make visible the social interactional medium in which cognition and learning might be taking place in classroom conversation" with a critical sensibility about the "ecosystem of relations of mutual influence between speakers who are also hearers and viewers" (p. 54). Based on the data presented, he asserts the importance of the role of time in interactional engagement. Grounding his assertion in an analysis of rhythms in the communication of the participants in the classroom in focus, Erickson states that "*time*, especially the cadential patterns produced by points of emphasis in the verbal and nonverbal behavior stream" (p. 54) function as contextualization cues for the players in the scene. He states, "As participants orient their attention and action to a common temporal framework, their contributions in listening and speaking behavior occur together, and interaction proceeds smoothly and coherently" (p. 55). This argument sets the scene for his discussion of turn sharks—those students who are able to discern patterns in speech acts and insert themselves (in place of their peers) into a teacher-student interaction—as well as several other behaviors that might be analyzed quite differently using another set of analytical lenses.

## FROM ARGUMENT TO ANALYSIS  ☆

It is worth noting how previous literature on talk, participation, turn-taking, and conversation analysis (among others) formed the building blocks for Erickson's approach to data analysis in "Going for the Zone." This analytic work is inductive, but the tools he used to *do* the work were provided by previous theory. Erickson's work is therefore instructive in terms of understanding the role of a conceptual framework in specific data analysis choices—that is, in how he actually went about reanalyzing his data in light of the set of theories he was using at this juncture.

The argument outlined above (paragraphs 1–14) constitutes the first half of Erickson's conceptual framework: he has made the case for why the topic matters. The next task is to show that he has developed a valid and rigorous approach to studying it. Because this chapter focuses on data analysis, the second set of excerpts and figures (paragraphs 15–24) show how the analysis followed the argument for the topic. To back his argument with data, Erickson needed to accomplish two things. First, he needed to identify an instance in the data where a ZPD could have developed (or was developing) in order to show the complications involved in doing so. This raises a difficult analytic problem: how to identify characteristics of a situation in which a ZPD could occur, and how to use those characteristics to locate such instances within the data. In other words, the characteristics of the ZPD had to be operationalized as analytic themes—descriptors that could be applied to the data. In this analysis, he used two criteria to identify a scenario in which a ZPD could be established. Broadly, there must be an interaction that involves an expert and a novice (per Vygotsky's theory). Further, it must be clear that within the interaction there is intent on the part of the expert to engage the novice. Drawing on his own and his colleagues' work on interaction analysis, Erickson uses the occurrence of a "known information question" to identify such a moment. The student is being asked the question at the same time as the desired response is indicated. This, Erickson argues, amounts to an invitation of the student, Angie, to take and hold the floor along with the teacher.

Having located an instance within the data in which a teacher and student were "going for the zone," Erickson was next required to show how actually establishing it was fraught with complexity. Because he had argued that understanding interaction meant understanding timing, making this point required that he demonstrate for the reader how the timing of this interaction complicated any efforts to establish or sustain a ZPD. More specifically, he needed to show how both *kairos* and *chronos* time, along with contextualization cues, could be seen within this process. To accomplish this, Erickson introduced two methodological innovations in his analysis and presentation of the data: the first was a unique transcription process designed to show the cadence of the conversation, and the second was a system of musical notation to show its precise rhythm.

## ☆ TRANSCRIPTION AS DATA ANALYSIS

For most researchers, transcription is simply the process through which recorded words are turned into printed words. Its neutrality is something that even many experienced researchers take for granted, believing that and acting as if it is a neutral act, as if anyone would organize the words and pauses in the same way. It therefore is typically viewed as a mechanical act (one that is often outsourced to professional services) rather than as a subjective and engaged one that holds within it layers of interpretation and that generates meanings based on these interpretations. This matters more for some types of analysis than others; for those who closely study interaction, the nuances of language, expression, and participation matter a great deal. Referring to a paper written by a colleague, Erickson explained:

> Even when you have an audiotape and a videotape, and you think you are being just a brute empiricist in transcribing the sounds, you are making choices in the way you arrange it on the page. And all that is foregrounding some things and backgrounding others. And so it is not theoretically neutral at all.

In some research, this point might be understood as a critique. For Erickson, it represents an opportunity. Taking a theoretical approach to transcription—deliberately emphasizing aspects of what is being transcribed in order to examine them more closely—is not preparation for data analysis but analysis itself. This is first evident in the excerpt in paragraphs 16 and 17, in which Erickson details a unique set of transcription conventions designed to draw out the cadence of the interactions he analyzes.

Before presenting the transcript, a brief summary of transcription conventions is appropriate:

> Transcription is done in breath group units rather than in whole lines horizontally across the page. Usually there are two lines per breath group, with the *tonal nucleus,* the syllable receiving primary volume and pitch stress, appearing at the left margin. Even more special stress on a syllable or word is indicated by an underline. (Such transcription by breath group, with the tonal nucleus made visually prominent, enables

the reader to read the text aloud and get a sense of the cadence organization that obtains within and between turns at speaking.)

Occasionally, when a second speaker begins to talk in response to a prior speaker, the second speaker's first word begins just to the right of the last word uttered by the prior speaker, as at (29–31) and (64–66).

Overlapping speech is indicated by this symbol: [

Alternation between speakers with no gap and no overlap ("latching") is indicated by this symbol: $\Sigma$ (pp. 38–39).

The effect of this approach is striking. In reading the transcript aloud, one can identify where words were emphasized, which words were stressed, and where speakers overlapped. By using transcription to show these aspects of communication to the reader, Erickson is able to explain in theoretical terms their significance. He shows how, through contextualization cues, the teacher created an opportunity for Angie (and Angie alone) to respond to a known information question (paragraphs 17 and 18). When she failed to respond in appropriate time to those cues, the "turn sharks"—other students who intuitively understood the cadence and knew the correct answer—interceded.

The transcription conventions used for this segment of analysis are highly effective in showing that there was a "right" time to respond to the teacher's questions, but they provide less information about how participants knew precisely when that right time occurred. For this, Erickson adopts another innovation in his treatment of transcription: He sets it to music. As shown in Figure 5.1 (between paragraphs 21 and 22), the turn sharks' timing was informed not just by contextualization cues such as the teacher's posture or gaze but by the actual rhythm of the conversation. For those who can read musical notation (or better yet, sound it out), this approach allows the reader to see (and hear) the precise sequence of teacher utterances and gestures, pauses, and student responses. Having presented the transcript as such, Erickson then shows that correct answers were continually and consistently provided one beat after the question, with stressed words in both question and response falling on that beat (paragraphs 21 and 22). These interactions effectively established the tempo of the interaction. Like a musician in an ensemble missing an entrance, he argues, Angie's failure to respond "in time" to the teacher's question about the letter *S* cued the other students that this was the time to cut in to the conversation (paragraphs 23 and 24).

This approach to data analysis is creative, but more than that, it is functional. Erickson's argument about the complexity of interaction—and thus complications in establishing a ZPD—relies on being able to show the reader that *time matters* when studying interaction. In this excerpt, we can see the utility of both identifying contextualization cues and of plotting transcript data onto a musical score. Erickson visually maps out the "rhythmic organization of questions and answers about school and letter name" (p. 46) by providing us with an innovative way to consider the data. This was a departure from much of the discourse analysis that was being done at the time, which tended to focus more heavily on the semantic links between turns within the interaction. "It is so much more complicated than that," Erickson reflected.

> [Timing] needed to be foregrounded in . . . transcribing. . . . By then I was transcribing with stressed syllables on the left margin, and then the little things that are going up to the next one on the right side, which doesn't look like conversation analysis, or anybody else's transcribing. That was an original thing of mine to emphasize this regularity of pulse, or cadence. And then, if you know how to read music, the quasimusical notation makes that even clearer.

It is worth noting that this innovation represents something of a theoretical fusion in itself. Erickson's knowledge of music theory and notation—designed as it is to plot sound (and silence) across time and participants—equipped him with a set of tools from well outside his disciplinary background that nonetheless furthered his analytic work. Equally important is the way this approach took shape. Theoretical developments led Erickson to believe that timing mattered, which in turn gave rise to methodological innovations. Reflecting on the evolution of this approach, Erickson explained:

> Particularly for Angie, the whole business of how adjacent turns get set up as matter of interactional sociolinguistics, or interactional accomplishment, is what led me to the close look at the timing of all this. And that's what led me ultimately to the musical notation stuff. Because by then I had looked at a lot of this kind of footage with that perspective, and I had written a couple of papers on the timing of adjacent turns. And it's the very time cues in shifts in postural position, gesture, gaze, and stressed syllables in the speech stream that help people . . . recognize that there's an underlying pulse here. Not consciously, but that there is an underlying pulse, or cadence. And it's the very regularity of that cadence that enables the turn sharks to know where to go to answer for, and also in the later scene. It is just exactly that issue of the real-time interactional performance dynamics of turn exchange.

This whole discussion about transcription conventions and the mapping of transcription data onto nonconventional structures (musical scores) tells a story of making analytical choices and the implications thereof for the building of specific data-based arguments. Erickson shares with his readers his choices around the structural and spatial organization of the actual words on the page. He provides a rationale and context for these choices that begins to map out his argument concerning the timing and cadence of speech and their complex relationship to engagement and perception in this classroom setting. This shows Erickson's careful analysis of the activity and speech acts in this classroom context, or what he refers to as "the ecology of social interaction" (p. 49) in this space and time.

## EVOLVING AND SHIFTING ☆ FRAMEWORKS OF ANALYSIS

"Going for the Zone" is a particularly compelling example of the role of a conceptual framework in data analysis because it shows how a researcher draws upon, as he enters into layered critical dialogue with, multiple intersecting fields that bear on the phenomena under study. While Erickson's work in general crosses a range of fields and disciplines, in the case of this chapter, these fields include sociolinguistics, discourse analysis, neo-Vygotskianism, social interaction theory, music theory, teacher research, and theories of culture and communication broadly. His engagement with these fields spans over four decades and becomes instantiated in a multilayered, creatively interdisciplinary approach to making sense of these specific data. It also evolved along with his continuing analysis and theoretical developments in related fields. Erickson's longstanding engagement in framework development that is iterative and reflexive allows us to understand the ways in which analysis is a conceptually embedded process, one that can shift and change as one's theoretical lenses and conceptual framing shifts over time.

Throughout his career as a researcher, Erickson has cultivated a critical and receptive sensibility about developing theory and theorizing practice, particularly in classroom settings. He structured his argument in this chapter around the concept of "social interaction as a learning environment" (p. 29), taking the conceptual core of neo-Vygotskian theory and framing it in a particular way using theories from across fields to address issues of communication and interaction in thinking, learning, and teaching.

"Going for the Zone" focuses on data that Erickson has actually analyzed at multiple points over the course of his career, using many different theoretical frames to make a variety of arguments within and across fields. This chapter, with its use of pre-existing data analyzed in new ways, brings to the fore the significance of how (and why) his reading and understanding of this conversation segment has changed over time. This helps us to understand the value of his own experience of learning and coming to know Vygotskian theory and the idea of the ZPD, as well as how it has shaped his critique of the assumption that the structure of the interaction is dyadic. This is crucial to understanding how he framed the data in this chapter, how this framing shaped and informed his thinking, in what respects he found these ideas (or their subsequent treatment in the literature) problematic, and how he thought these concepts could (and should) be reconfigured based on that assessment. This in turn helps us to understand what he was hoping to interject into the conversation about classroom interaction: the complexity of classroom ecologies and how context, timing, and relational and communicative rhythms shape actions within this setting.

Erickson's long experience with these specific data, coupled with the theoretical and intellectual evolution of the fields in which he has worked (described above) offer us a unique perspective on how the analysis of data changes as one's conceptual framework evolves. He made meaning of these data in various ways that fit within the intellectual and theoretical milieux of the time, even as he informed them through his own work. His integration (and critique) of neo-Vygotskian theory was the latest in a series of shifts in how he viewed the data.

> I'd had all these . . . sociolinguistic interests from the earlier times. And as I sat there watching the tape—and I had used this in my teaching about classroom life, so the issue of the turn sharks had come up as we watched it. . . . One reason I took this clip was that I knew that there was stuff in it that I could show people, and it had intrinsic interest. And then, as I was working up the presentation . . . [one] way of thinking about this is that this little conversation is a kind of interrupted zone of proximal development.

This recollection evokes our discussion from Chapter 2 about the meaning of theory, and why it can be so difficult to understand and to define. Of course, theory refers to how things relate to one another, but it also serves as a lens through which you view your world and your work. Shifting theoretical orientations necessitate shifts in conceptual framework; paragraphs 1 through 14 are the consequence of such a shift. But more important, these shifts change what you see in your data, both in terms of which specific data grab your attention and how you make sense of their meaning. For example, Erickson explained how the lens of neo-Vygotskian theory directed his attention to certain events and characters within his data.

> If it hadn't been Vygotsky, it might have been critical ethnography. . . . It would have been then a very different story. The data would have been

different, what was foregrounded would have been different, and [another student] would have been in the center of the story, and Angie and her gear-shifting problems would maybe not even [have] been mentioned.

We find this explanation of his approach to analyzing the data in terms of his choices about how to situate and frame his analysis an important one, particularly given the confusion surrounding the choice of conceptual frameworks and the influence of those choices on data analysis. It is striking that Erickson's consideration of a new theoretical framework led him to view, or review, the data differently, to see new and different things in them, and to recast his argument in an innovative direction. This speaks to the multiple influences on interpretive frames and analytical arguments; it helps us see the power and implications of conceptual framing. This can teach us a great deal about how conceptual frameworks inform analytic themes or categories (and vice versa) as well as about how one's working theoretical frames influence quite specific moments of data reduction, organization, and analysis.

If the emphasis is going to be on turn sharks, then turn-taking and its interactional enactment, and all the things that go into that, are what you end up focusing on analytically. . . . You see different things in the videotape when you have these different orienting concerns, which is part of the point.

There is a subjectivity to this processes—the intertwined nature of what we think about and what we see—that may initially make you uncomfortable. Does this simply mean that we look for confirmation of our pre-existing views within the data? It does not. Rather, it points to the relationship between deductive and inductive analysis. In Erickson's analysis of the role of time and timing in structuring conversation, much of the analysis is inductive—the data direct his attention to the argument. But his evolving sense of its significance, both academically and educationally, was continually recast by theory and thus shifted the structure and contextualization of that argument—essentially a deductive process. "There is a real place for a more inductive way of coming to whatever theoretical frameworks you can use," he explained.

And my story is very much that way of going back and forth with something like data, but also as your theoretical interests change, what you see changes. . . . You can't just say "Well, I'm a poststructuralist, therefore. . . ." It seems to me beginners make [that] mistake. Some of them make the mistake of thinking that you can just be completely atheoretical— and that's naïve. But the other naïveté is to think that somehow there's some book someplace that's got the theory in it, that's then going to [tell you what to do].

This statement is an important one about the nature of one's mind-set going into empirical research. Erickson is speaking about the complex relationship between understanding the theoretical and conceptual frameworks that guide us and remaining open to what emerges from the data. This requires that you understand the relationship between *framing theories* and *emergent theories*, among other things. We argue that this tension is a generative one. The ways that emergent theory maps onto, relates with, and challenges preconceived theoretical frameworks are what allow you to critically and appropriately develop data-based theories (Anderson & Jones, 2000; Bailey & Jackson, 2003; Chawla, 2006; Jaffee et al., 1999).

Finally, it is worth noting that in keeping with themes from the previous two chapters, there is something of an autobiographical aspect to Erickson's approach to analysis. This is candidly acknowledged in the text of the article when he explains that "the heavier emphasis on interaction than on cognition in this chapter is due to the focal interests of its author" (p. 56). But there is a more fine-grained aspect to this formulation that speaks more deeply to the link between who we are and what we find important or interesting. "The more I think about it, the more I'm persuaded that the central focus of one's work in social inquiry, the crucial problems that you focus on in your career, are fundamentally autobiographical," he commented.

> In my case, my earlier work on gatekeeping interaction, and the assessments that people make of each other and their capacities, that was an issue that as a young man I was very anxious about. . . . I know that judgments about "Other" is something that was a front-burner issue for me. And I managed to do some good stuff with that. But it wasn't taking that off the shelf, at all. . . . Ultimately, it isn't that you pick a theory, and then pick a site, and then come out with a study that could be predicted by knowing what you reached for on the shelf.

This personal statement about how Erickson gravitated to the central topics of his career, as well as about his teaching of generations of doctoral students and discerning the personal influences on their work, is meant to provoke a particular kind of research reflexivity: an identification of and reckoning with the autobiographical aspects of one's interest in and commitment to particular lines of inquiry. Echoing Michelle Fine's comments from the previous chapter, Erickson explained that the important thing is to be clear about those preferences, to acknowledge them forthrightly, and ultimately to use them to delve more deeply into the work:

Rather than being an open window on somebody else's world, unedited video footage like this, when people watch it, works like a projective test. It's like a Rorschach inkblot. You read into it whatever's on your front burner. I'm sure this is true for any kind of evidence, but particularly for video, there's so much potential information there. It's so dense with information bits that you can't extract data out of them. That is, paying attention to some information bits rather than others, you have to do that, because otherwise it would just be totally incoherent. It's the buzzing and blooming confusion that William James talked about. So, it's got to be selective attention. And the best you can do is try to disprove your favorite hunches about what's going on by looking over and over very carefully.

## CONCEPTUAL FRAMEWORKS AND DATA ☆ ANALYSIS: CONCLUDING THOUGHTS

As this chapter presents, data analysis and theory development are ideally in an iterative and dynamic relationship. We argue that the degree to which a researcher views these as a "dialectic of mutual influence" (Nakkula & Ravitch, 1998) is directly related to the quality of your analysis. Frederick Erickson's reflections on "Going for the Zone" show clearly how the arguments that we make inform our choices about what to focus on within the data and how to analyze those data. Beyond that, the story presented in this chapter illuminates the relationship between theoretical and conceptual frameworks. In this instance, a shift in theoretical framework—using neo-Vygotskian theory to analyze how learning happens in a classroom situation—opened up new analytic possibilities but also revealed shortcomings in the theory itself, shortcomings that the author attempted to both illuminate and address through specific analytic methods. Articulating the logical connection between the problem identified (in this case, the inattention to the complexity of interaction in the theoretical framework) and the methodological means to address it (analyzing the role of timing within such interactions) is a central function of conceptual frameworks. Though they may evolve along with our theoretical understandings and methodological innovations, their role in anchoring those developments to fundamental arguments about what we study and how we study remains constant. The extension of those arguments—explaining to the reader why what we have learned is important, and what its implications are—is where the conceptual framework is culminated. It is to this final stage, presenting and contextualizing findings, that we turn in the next chapter.

☆ READING REFERENCES

Auer, P. (1992). Introduction: John Gumperz' approach to contextualization. In P. Auer & A. Di Luzio (Eds.), *The contextualization of language* (pp. 1–37). Amsterdam: John Benjamins.

Bateson, G. (1956). The message "This is a play." In B. Schaffner (Ed.), *Group processes*. New York: Josiah Macy, Jr., Foundation.

Cooper-Kuhlen, E. (1992). Contextualizing discourse: The prosody of interactive repair. In P. Auer & A. Di Luzio (Eds.), *The contextualization of language* (pp. 337–364). Amsterdam: John Benjamins.

Erickson, F. (1982). Money tree, lasagna bush, salt and pepper: Social construction of topical cohesion in a conversation among Italian-Americans. In D. Tannen (Ed.), *Analyzing discourse: Text and talk* (pp. 43–70). Washington, DC: Georgetown University Press.

Erickson, F. (1986). Listening and speaking. In D. Tannen & J. Alatis (Eds.), *Georgetown University Roundtable in Languages and Linguistics 1985*. Washington, DC: Georgetown University Press.

Erickson, F. (1992). They know all the lines: Rhythmic organization and contextualization in a conversational listing routine. In P. Auer & A. Di Luzio (Eds.) *The contextualization of language* (pp. 365–397). Amsterdam: John Benjamins.

Erickson, F., & Shultz, J. (1982). *The counselor as gatekeeper: Social interaction in interviews*. New York: Academic Press.

Gumperz, J. J. (1982). *Discourse strategies*. Cambridge, UK: Cambridge University Press.

Hammersley, M., & Atkinson, P. (2007). *Ethnography*. New York: Routledge.

Heath, S. B. (1983). *Ways with words: Language, life and work in communities and classrooms*. Cambridge, UK: Cambridge University Press.

Scollon, R. (1982). The rhythmic integration of ordinary talk. In D. Tannen & J. Alatis (Eds.), *Georgetown University Roundtable on Languages and Linguistics*. Washington, DC: Georgetown University Press.

Vygotsky, L. S. (1978). *Mind in society: The development of higher psychological processes*. (M. Cole, V. John-Steiner, S. Scribner, & E. Souberman, Eds.). Cambridge, MA: Harvard University Press.

Wertsch, J. V. (1985). *Culture, communication, and cognition: Vygotskian perspectives*. Cambridge, UK: Cambridge University Press.

Wood, D., Bruner, J. S., & Ross, G. (1976). The role of tutoring in problem solving. *Journal of Child Psychology and Psychiatry*, *17*, 89–100.

CHAPTER 6

# EXPANDING THE CONVERSATION, EXTENDING THE ARGUMENT

## *The Role of Conceptual Frameworks in Presenting, Explaining, and Contextualizing Findings*

In traditional scientific literature, the relationship between theory and results is often portrayed as linear: either the data support the hypothesis or they do not. From this perspective, the relationship between one's conceptual framework and findings seems straightforward. In social science research, however, hypotheses are more like interwoven threads in a complex tapestry; it is difficult if not impossible to pull on one without pulling on several others. The most ardent of positivists would chafe at this type of complexity, because without isolating the phenomena or processes in question, it is difficult to determine causality. But social phenomena are inherently multifaceted and complex, and the vast majority of social science research is not conducted under laboratory conditions. As such, findings seldom conform neatly to expectations, nor are they linear or easily isolated. Because of this, you are left with the difficult and sometimes ambiguous task of making sense of what you have learned. Unlike the scientific archetype in which results are analyzed primarily (or only) in relation to specific hypotheses, this process often involves a thoughtful interrogation of the assumptions and logic that led to your results. Conceptual frameworks help you to contextualize and make sense of your findings, but you also use findings to review, revise, and, ultimately, strengthen your conceptual framework.

This type of recursive relationship between theory and data is common in qualitative research. Conceptual frameworks shape a study's design and research questions, but answers to those questions are often drawn out through inductive (rather than deductive) data analysis. In this sense, dialectic is established between the theoretical constructs that framed the study and those that emerge from it.

Often overlooked, however, is that the same dialectic exists in quantitative research. While most quantitative work relies on constructs that are established a priori (prior to analysis), the relationships between those constructs—the links in the conceptual framework—are dynamic and often unpredictable. The surprises generated through data analysis contribute to the understanding of the phenomena under review, but also beg the question of what generated those surprises to begin with. Were your assumptions flawed? Were there constructs that should have been included but were not? Were there critical processes that you overlooked? This type of questioning is critical to your continued learning as a researcher. Ultimately, these surprises help you to advance your own work and contribute to a broader understanding of the topics and issues you choose to study.

The process of working back and forth between conceptual frameworks and findings, and the way this process shapes your writing, is the focus of this chapter. Our discussion focuses on the pathbreaking work of Margaret Beale Spencer. Specifically, we review and discuss "A Phenomenological Variant of Ecological Systems Theory (PVEST): A Self-Organization Perspective in Context," written with Davido Dupree and Tracey Hartmann. We chose to focus on this specific piece for two reasons. First, it relies exclusively on quantitative methods, which makes it unique among the works featured in this book. Second, it is, among other things, a story of what can happen when researchers encounter surprises in their data, and how they deal with those discoveries.

## ABOUT THE AUTHOR ☆

Margaret Beale Spencer is the Marshall Field IV Professor of Urban Education in the Department of Comparative Human Development at the University of Chicago. Previously, as the Board of Overseers Professor of Interdisciplinary Studies in Human Development at the University of Pennsylvania, she was also the Director of the W. E. B. Du Bois Collective Research Institute as well as the Center for Health Achievement Neighborhood Growth and Ethnic Studies (CHANGES). Spencer's Phenomenological Variant of Ecological Systems Theory (PVEST) addresses life-course development and serves as the foundation for her race/ethnicity- and gender-acknowledging developmental research. The programmatic human development effort addresses resiliency, identity, and competence formation processes for ethnically diverse groups (particularly African American, Hispanic, Asian American, and European American youth) who reside in neighborhoods with varied resources. Her continuing research and programming applications address youths' emerging capacity for healthy outcomes and constructive coping methods while developing under unacknowledged and stressful conditions. She has published approximately 120 articles and chapters since 1973, completed three edited volumes, and received funding for more than three dozen research proposals from foundations and federal agencies. Most recently, she was awarded the 2006 Fletcher Fellowship, which recognized work that furthers the broad social goals of the U.S. Supreme Court's *Brown v. Board of Education* decision of 1954. She joined the faculty of the Department of Comparative Human Development and The College of the University of Chicago in 2009.

## BACKGROUND AND CONTEXT: ☆
## AN OVERVIEW OF THE WORK IN FOCUS

For decades, researchers exploring the relationship between economic poverty and life outcomes have struggled with something of a paradox. On the one hand, economic poverty affects just about everything else, from income to life expectancy, and in most cases does so more than any other identifiable factor. On the other hand, within high-poverty populations, the range of life outcomes for any individual varies considerably. Economic poverty shapes people's lives, but it does not determine them. This raises an intriguing and important question: What is it that allows some people to successfully negotiate the obstacles presented by economic poverty while others do not? Which social, community, or individual characteristics help people to cope with these challenges, and which ones make it harder for them to do so?

This basic question has long been at the core of Margaret Beale Spencer's research. The present article, "A Phenomenological Variant of Ecological Systems Theory (PVEST): A Self-Organization Perspective in Context," is an outgrowth of a much longer (and continuing) line of research. While this line of inquiry has been conducted in multiple contexts using different types of data and with a variety of collaborators, the unifying thread has been Spencer's pioneering of the PVEST. A full rendering of the origins and components of this theoretical framework would require an entire chapter in itself (see Spencer, 2008; Spencer et al., 2006), but it is important to understand its basic premise and lineage.

As the name implies, PVEST fuses a theory of development (ecological systems theory) with a phenomenological perspective on the processes through which development occurs. As articulated by developmental psychologist Urie Bronfenbrenner (1979), Ecological Systems Theory maintains that human development is profoundly influenced by a nested set of systems ranging from the intimate to the removed. Put simply, Bronfenbrenner argues that development is a function of the individual's interactions with *microsystems* such as family, neighborhood, and school. These microsystems interact with and thereby mutually influence one another inside a *mesosystem*, which is in turn situated within an *exosystem*—the wider social settings in which *microsystems* are situated, such as personal or professional networks or direct interactions with organizations or institutions. These settings are themselves nested within a *macrosystem* in which economic, social, and cultural influences form the context inhabited by all of the other systems. Changes in any of these systems affect the smaller systems that reside within them, and ultimately the development of the individual. As Bronfenbrenner explains, ecological systems theory

> seeks to provide a unified but highly differentiated conceptual scheme for describing and interrelating structures and processes in both the immediate and more remote environment as it shapes the course of human development throughout the lifespan. (p. 11)

While Bronfenbrenner (1979) stresses that it is the perceived characteristics of the environment (as opposed to an "objective" reality) that are most salient to development—and designs his research accordingly—the processes and interactions through which those perceptions are formed, and the ways in which those processes influence development, are not a primary focus in his empirical work. In her research, Spencer seeks to better understand these processes and to interrogate and learn about how interactions and experiences shape individuals' understanding of the world and their place within it. It was this interest that led to the incorporation of a phenomenological perspective into her research. While phenomenology, a branch of philosophy concerned with the nature of phenomena, has been employed in the social and behavioral sciences in a variety of ways, Spencer uses the term in a manner most commonly found in psychology. Phenomenological psychology holds that people's experiences cannot be observed objectively; rather, they can only be understood on their own terms within a person's broader meaning making and rendering of their experiences in the world (Langdridge, 2007). From a phenomenological perspective, the process of making meaning of these experiences is intersubjective; that is, their significance is shaped through the interaction and mutual influence of individual, subjective impressions of shared experience (Nakkula & Ravitch, 1998).

In sum, PVEST accepts the person-environment logic of development that is at the core of Ecological Systems Theory, but focuses on processes underlying development rather than its outcomes. As Spencer (2008) asserts:

> The conceptual combination of phenomenology with ecological systems perspectives serves to improve one's appreciation of the "how" of development. Emphasizing the "how" of development is very different from the traditional and linear acknowledging of the "what" (i.e. individuals' patterned outcomes). (p. 698)

This fitting together of theories—literally a theoretical framework—led Spencer to develop two new propositions that are central to PVEST. First, the work of making sense of both self and environment coalesces over time into a stable identity, which in turn rationalizes behavior (whether adaptive or maladaptive). Second, the process of identity formation is bidirectional. Behavior has outcomes and consequences for the individual, but at the same time it also affects other people, and thus alters the environment in which sense making and identity formation occur. Each of these propositions has real implications for our understanding of the broader relationship between life circumstances and outcomes. *Resiliency*, often thought of as some innate quality or characteristic, takes on a different meaning when viewed through a PVEST framework; it is as likely to be found in the environment surrounding the individual—which provides the experiences that must be interpreted and integrated with a sense of self—as in the individual herself.

## BEING IN CONVERSATION WITH THEORY: ☆ INFLUENCES ON THOUGHT AND ACTION

When you develop a conceptual framework, you position yourself in relation to existing bodies of literature as well as theories already in place. As noted in Chapter 1, this process of developing the conceptual framework of a study is often imagined as a conversation; the question is the degree to which you choose to insert yourself into that conversation—what in this book we have discussed as a conversation already happening—and how you make your entrance. Margaret Beale Spencer chose to enter the conversation forcefully. At the core of PVEST is a strident critique of earlier theories of human development, one borne out of personal experience as well as prior and ongoing scholarship.

In our interview with her, Spencer shared some of the personal experiences that influenced both her broad career trajectory and her specific research agenda. An African American female, Spencer was raised in an underresourced urban Philadelphia neighborhood in the 1950s, primarily by her mother, who modeled particular values and socialized her daughters to share those values. Mrs. Elizabeth R. Beale impressed upon her daughters that much was expected of them and that each had every capacity to live up to those expectations. Margaret noticed from an early age that the initial primary school she attended did not share her family's lofty expectations. "My mother inculcated particular values and expectations concerning hard work and responsibility," she recalled. "I attended school but wasn't really impressed. I was experiencing dissonance around assumptions concerning race, socioeconomic status [SES], as well as expectations." Spencer intuitively began to develop a sensibility around the mismatch between home and school, specifically as it related to expectations for African American students and families. This was a defining experience of her K–12 years and left her with questions and goals in relation to issues of race, equity, and identity. She has made a career out of answering these questions and in so doing has contributed a great deal to our understanding of this area of psychoeducational research.

Spencer completed a master's degree at the University of Kansas before pursuing doctoral studies at the University of Chicago. Spencer found that the pathologization of African American children was equally prevalent in the academic world as in the K–12 sphere. Theories of human development, she found, were riddled with assumptions about race, social class, and gender. Specifically, whiteness was generally assumed to be "normal" and deviations from whiteness therefore pathological (Spencer et al., 2006). Once again Spencer experienced a troubling dissonance, this time between what she was reading about African American children and what she experienced on a daily basis. As she stated in her interview,

Here I was as a doctoral student, raising children, studying development, while also asking questions about normal human development for diverse youngsters, which were not in the textbooks. The textbooks were basically biased in the sense that they made a priori assumptions based upon ethnicity, race, SES, and skin color. Thus, there were no alternatives for me except to challenge those assumptions.

The present article uses the PVEST framework to explore a specific aspect of development: self-organization. In the psychology literature, the process of self-organization essentially describes how identity forms. There are two reasons why it was important to link the broader theoretical framework to this specific concept. First, self-organization describes the cultivation of a relatively stable sense of self through which both experience and responses to those experiences are filtered. This is consistent with PVEST, which argues that stable identities are the cumulative coping product of repeated interactions between the person and the environment. Second, as the authors refer to it in this article, self-organization has specific implications for resiliency. One's identity, Spencer and her colleagues argue, has significant bearing on whether a young person responds to challenging circumstances in what she conceives of as adaptive or maladaptive ways. Linking concepts of self-organization to PVEST roots the concept more firmly in the literature while simultaneously advancing the argument that identity processes are central to human development.

While this chapter focuses primarily on how Spencer contextualized and explained the results of her research in light of the article's conceptual framework, a brief summary of the data and methodology employed is important to understanding those results. Because they are best understood in light of the article's conceptual framework, we insert a summary of the data, methods, and results in between two excerpts from the article, the first of which outlines the argument and the second of which discusses the results.

Spencer, M., Dupree, D., & Hartmann, T. (1997). A Phenomenological Variant of Ecological Systems Theory (PVEST): A self-organizational perspective in context. *Development and Psychopathology*, *9*, 817–833; Reprinted with the permission of Cambridge University Press.

## Comparisons of PVEST and Self-Organization Perspectives

[1] Cicchetti and Tucker (1994) emphasize the "individual's active strivings for self-organization as the major determinant of ontogenesis." For them, self-organization leads development from "a state of relative globality and lack of differentiation to a state of increasing differentiation, integration, articulation and hierarchic integration." Resilience is defined from the self-organizational perspective as the "ability to utilize self-righting tendencies" during sensitive periods or in response to negative feedback as in Cicchetti et al.'s (1993) study of maltreated children

(Cicchetti & Tucker, 1994, p. 534). For instance, a youth who is generally perceived as quiet and withdrawn may similarly think of himself as shy. However, with more experiences, interactions, and feedback in different contexts, the child may develop a more differentiated understanding of himself. The youth may recognize the contexts (e.g., people, places, activities) in which he is more quiet and reflective versus those contexts where he is more outgoing and engaging. Consequently, the youth develops his ability to use self-righting tendencies such as avoiding certain people, places, or activities, downplaying or emphasizing the importance or value of certain people, places, or activities. The youth may even learn how to capitalize on the perception of being quiet and reflective when it is associated with other traits that are valuable in different contexts. For instance, a child of few words who is also above average in size compared to peers may not need to be particularly verbose if physical stature is associated with fighting or athletic ability. On the other hand, in a classroom: setting, an African-American female of few words may be perceived as a good student merely because she is not a behavior problem. The point is that self-organization is determined not only by context (e.g., home, school, community) but by the phenomenological experience of race, gender, physical status, and many other potential factors.

[2] According to Lewis (1995), emotional and/or cognitive appraisals of the environment influence the moment to moment patterns of self organization. Stability in an individual is recognized when situational response patterns become personality structures. Change in the self-system is explained by perturbations in the life of the individual. These perturbations include changes in the environment or the individual such as cognitive development or puberty. Significant perturbations or those that occur at particularly sensitive periods cause disequilibrium. New experiences—including new thoughts and emotions—must be integrated. The PVEST expands on this self-organization perspective by nesting the self in the larger micro- and macro-systems and illuminating the impact of feedback from the environment, particularly related to individual differences of race, class, skin color, gender, and maturational differences. The emphasis provides a more enhanced interpretation of interactive effects of culture and context with life-span ontogenesis.

### Environmental risks/stress engagement: Perturbations/negative feedback to the system

[3] Recurring experiences of the same feedback and stress can cause the individual to repeatedly reorganize in response to environmental

conditions. Feedback and repeated response patterns would crystallize into personality structures, particular developmental trajectories, and identity. What does this mean if the individual is living in, as Chestang (1972) states, a hostile environment, experiencing chronic and negative feedback loops and the stress of poverty and violence on a daily basis? Lewis (1995) offers that when an individual receives negative feedback, the use of a defense mechanism is required for the individual to continue functioning in a way that does not threaten his or her ability to see him or herself as valued in different contexts. Thus, African-American students experiencing negative feedback about the self in school might shut off from this critically important experience. This decision may result in the diverting of psychic energy and attention to their peer group and reorganizing themselves or more closely attaching to a group which provides positive, or at least less threatening, feedback. The decision—which could lead to problem behaviors, school drop-out, and delinquency—may be of help in the short term in preserving the self, although exponentially troubling efforts for mastery and competence in the long term. Consequently, behaviors that may lead to resilient appearing outcomes in the short term, however, may lead to pathological outcomes in the long term. Pathology occurs when the self-system "shuts down" in a sense, becomes reactively organized around negative feedback about the self, does not fully integrate all components, or becomes dependent upon maladaptive solutions as "self-righting tendencies" as its major corrective problem-solving strategy. This differs from effective coping—the use of adaptive solutions as one's corrective problem-solving strategy; when repetitively used as stable coping responses, the outcome is an achieved identity or set of healthy psychosocial processes that undergird the probability of productive life-stage coping products.

[4] As a demonstration of the PVEST model as an *extended* self-organizational perspective and as illustrated in Figure 6.1, in this paper we explore a model predicting negative academic learning attitude. The model includes a particular risk (female headship) and two levels of stress engagement. Female headship is believed to be a pre-existing risk contributor and is included in the model as a control for any possible differences based on family structure. The first level of stress engagement is a self-report of whether the adolescent experienced certain stressful events within the past year (stressful events). Cumulative stressful experiences have been found to have a synergistic effect which couples with other experiences that draw on the cognitive resources of adolescents; accordingly, it also was included in the model as a control to account for differences based on the number of

stressors one must deal with. The second level of stress engagement (perceived social supports) is more concerned with the phenomenological experience of stress and includes perceived positive teacher expectations for black males, perceived popularity with peers, and perceived unpopularity with peers. It is assumed that the less social support one perceives from teachers and peers, the more negative learning attitude one will exhibit as a stable coping response or

**Figure 6.1** Model of relationship among female headship, stressful events, perceived social supports, general positive attitude, and negative learning attitude

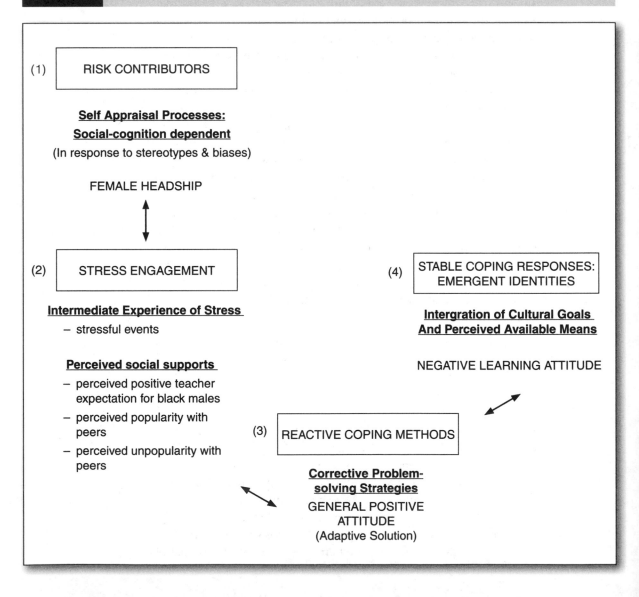

emergent identity. The model also includes an adaptive (vs. maladaptive) reactive coping method, generally positive attitude, suggested as a mediator variable (refer to Figure 6.1). It is assumed that a general positive attitude can mediate the relationship between perceived social supports (i.e., the source of stress) and negative learning attitude (i.e., the stable [psychosocial linked] coping response). That is, the higher the general positive attitude, the lower the negative learning attitude. Negative learning attitude represents an emergent identity in this model and stable coping response to stress. The assumption is that the adoption of a negative learning attitude emanates from the repetitive use of particular corrective problem-solving strategies: for example, involved is the frequent employment of maladaptive solutions or infrequent use of adaptive solutions (i.e., in this case infrequent use of a general positive attitude) in the face of perceived social supports or lack thereof. Accordingly, a negative learning attitude is suggested as a stable coping response or emergent identity that serves to maintain a "positive view of themselves" as perceived by particular adolescents. Importantly, the implications of a negative learning attitude as an emergent identity include a devaluing of learning activities as well as a diminished role of academics in such youths' experiences.

[5] Accordingly, the analyses explore two hypotheses. First, an *inverse* relationship is expected between having a general positive attitude and the stable (psychosocial) coping response: negative learning attitude. Second, for this sample of African-American adolescent males, specifically two of the perceived social support predictor variables (i.e., perceived positive teacher expectations for black males, and perceived unpopularity with peers) are expected to be significant contributors to the prediction of negative learning attitude; the direction of effects for the two variables (i.e., perceived positive teacher expectations for black males, and perceived unpopularity with peers) is expected to be negative and positive, respectively.

## Summary of Data, Methods, and Results

[6] The findings presented in this article are based upon an analysis of survey data from 266 African American students (181 male, 85 female) ages 14 to 17. The survey itself was compiled from well-established instruments that had been validated through prior research. The central variables discussed in the article—stressful events, perceived teacher perceptions, perceived popularity with peers, general positive attitude, and negative learning attitude—were each based on scales that had

themselves been tested and found reliable. Simple correlations were used to explore the strength of associations between variables; setwise regression was used to analyze the extent to which predictor variables (female headship, stressful life events, perceived popularity with peers, and general positive attitude) explained variance in the outcome of interest (negative learning attitude). Because PVEST hypothesizes that gender influences how young people interpret and respond to their lived experiences, the analyses were run separately for boys and girls.

[7] The analyses produced the following results:

1. For boys, experience of stressful life events was positively correlated ($r = .27, p <. 001$) with a general positive attitude. In other words, the more stressful events boys reported experiencing within the past year, the more positive their general attitude.

2. For boys, there was a negative correlation ($r = −.3, p < .001$) between stressful life events and a negative learning attitude.

3. Perceived unpopularity with peers was related to a less general positive attitude ($r = −.28, p < .001$ for boys; $r = −.21, p < .05$ for girls); and a more negative learning attitude ($r = .47, p < .001$ for boys; $r = .52, p < .001$ for girls).

4. For boys and girls, perceived unpopularity with peers explained the greatest percentage of variance in negative learning attitude.

5. For boys, perceived popularity with peers was a significant predictor of a less negative learning attitude ($\beta = −0.22, p < .01$). The same relationship did not exist for girls.

6. For boys, perceived positive teacher expectations for black males were associated with a less negative learning attitude, but the relationship was considerably weaker ($p < .10$) than for other mediating variables.

7. For boys and girls, female headship was not a significant predictor of negative learning attitude.

## Discussion

[8] As initially stated, one of the important strengths of coupling a phenomenological perspective with an ecological systems approach is that it affords a more dynamic, culturally responsive, context-sensitive perspective for interpreting the individual's own meaning making process: It captures the individual's intersubjectivity. The perspective

is particularly important for understanding the school experiences of African-American adolescents. The significant physical, cognitive, physiological, and emotional normative changes associated with ado lescence make the period, in and of itself, an unusual source of disequilibrium for a critical developmental transition as youth prepare themselves for a successful passage into adulthood. In American society, academic competence is an important foundational component for successful adulthood and, in fact, life course competence. Thus, experiences had in the school context that leave students feeling disfranchised and/or lead to school drop out or delinquency must be recognized. The school context continues to be a source of special challenge for youth of color and economically disadvantaged teens. Understanding youths' subjective processes and their relationship to academically significant outcomes are of critical importance (Fordham & Ogbu, 1986). Adolescent attitudes toward learning represent a critical outcome variable and was the criterion measure for the study in light of the long-recognized relationship between poor school performance and problem behaviors (e.g., Took & Weiss, 1994).

[9] All measures were student reports for self or student perceptions of teachers and peers. As indicated by Figure [6.1], in this paper we attempt to couple risk/stress variables with a reactive (although adaptive) coping method, general positive attitude, for the prediction of a stable coping response: negative learning attitude. In addition to stressful events, a set of perceived social support variables were included as other stress factors; perceived positive teacher expectation for Black males, perceived popularity with peers, and perceived unpopularity with peers (see Figure [6.1]).

[10] The general goal of the hypotheses tested was to explore the etiology of adolescents' negative learning attitudes. The first hypothesis explored the efficacy of the reactive coping method, general positive attitude, as a contributor variable in the prediction of negative learning attitude. The second hypothesis explored whether two of the three perceived social support variables (i.e., perceived positive teacher expectations for Black males and perceived unpopularity with peers) were the most salient in the prediction of negative learning attitude.

[11] Evident from Tables 3 and 4 [not included here] is that female headship was not a significant predictor for males or females. From a phenomenological perspective, family structure alone would not necessarily explain differences in psychological states such as negative learning attitudes. Rather, PVEST suggests that the self-appraisal processes that the adolescent makes with respect to his or her family's structure will have greater influence than the family structure itself.

Nevertheless, other factors were significant contributors in the prediction of negative learning attitude. For girls, as reported in Table 4, after controlling for risk and stressful events which were not significant, perceived unpopularity with peers was the single significant contributor to girls' negative learning attitude. Unexpected was that stress experienced was of total unimportance for negative teaming attitudes for girls given its unmistakable salience and consistent importance across steps of the regression for boys. Given the *singular* importance of unpopularity with peers for negative learning attitudes in the case of girls, on the one hand, the regression finding might suggest a special sensitivity to perceptions of unpopularity with peers for girls versus boys. On the other hand, the significance *of both* unpopularity and popularity with peers in predicting negative learning attitudes for boys might, in fact, suggest their broader and undifferentiated responsivity to peer evaluative feedback; importantly, it provides significant opportunities for intervention/prevention supports. Further, in the case of girls, if the stress measure had been heavily weighted for assessing *peer-specific* stress, might there have been an equally important predictive relationship between stress and negative learning attitude across the different steps? Perhaps the findings suggest broader, *generic* sources of importance (in fact, academically nonmarginalizing?) in the lives of males versus females. More physiologically and health-relevant theorizing concerning sex differences suggest greater undifferentiated and life-course associated vulnerability to stress for males when compared to females (Wingard, 1987). In fact, hypotheses about the greater longevity of females in general have been linked to their life course development and use of same-sex relationships as opposed to men's greater reliance on opposite-sex (i.e., marital) bonds. In sum, the salience of unpopularity and popularity with peers for boys and the singular significance of unpopularity with peers for girls might, in and of themselves, represent different etiologies.

[12] There were other interesting differences for boys (refer to Table 3). First, stressful life events were highly important for males in the prediction of negative learning attitudes in an unexpected direction: more stress was a significant predictor of a less negative learning attitude. Stressful life events continued to contribute across steps with a negative beta at each of the subsequent steps of the regression equation. The pattern may mean, as suggested, that boys who experience a significant amount of stress in their lives stay more engaged in the schooling process, are less marginalized and invisible and, consequently, have a less negative learning attitude. Although a qualitative analysis of experiences was not done, this unexpected predictive relationship might imply that for males, in particular, stressful events may be a proxy for the lack of marginalization.

That is, youth may be heavily engaged in social activities which also result in significant opportunities for stressful events. Certainly data obtained for girls suggest their greater classroom centrality when compared to Black males (see Irvine, 1990).

[13] Independent of gender, perceived social supports, specifically perceived unpopularity with peers, accounted for a significant amount of variance for youths' negative learning attitude. As suggested, over a third of the variance for negative learning attitude for girls was accounted for by the sole significant contributing variable: perceived unpopularity with peers (refer to Table 4). The prediction model for boys is especially important since it presents many more opportunities for intervention strategies and social supports. For example, reporting few significant life events may suggest marginalization and may be important in the acquisition of negative learning attitudes. Additionally, all three perceived social supports were significant contributors. Perceiving that teachers hold positive expectations for Black males is associated with less negative leaning attitudes. Similarly, a perception of being popular with peers is associated with a less negative learning attitude. On the other hand, like the findings for girls, the perception by boys that they are unpopular with peers is a significant predictor of negative learning attitude. Further, even though just marginally significant ($p < .05$) the reactive (adaptive) coping method, having a generally positive attitude, is related to a less negative learning attitude for boys (refer to Table 3).

[14] Resilience is only recognized in the context of adverse or stressful experiences. Having a generally positive attitude is suggested as an effective reactive (although adaptive) coping method. It is used as an adaptive corrective problem-solving strategy in the face of challenge which helps a person to move through the adverse circumstance through the use of a strategy, perhaps, that keeps one "upbeat" and positive. In fact, the findings for boys provide support for the first hypothesis that explored the importance of that coping method for learning attitude. The finding for boys, in fact, was in the expected (inverse) direction: less evident use of positive attitude as a reactive coping method is associated with a negative learning attitude. Consequently, the modest although significant contribution of a positive learning attitude to youths' negative learning attitude may suggest that, to some extent, boys have learned to perceive certain experiences—that would be highly stressful or discouraging for others—as a part of everyday experience (i.e., merely something else or one more challenge). There may be events that occur so consistently that some youth use reactive (adaptive) coping responses developed, adopted, and modeled by members of the community and which may for some, cast the experiences themselves in a more positive light. That is, the sheer prevalence of specific challenges prevents a

more personalized internalization of affect. On the other hand, other students may lack exposure to models who make frequent use of reactive coping methods that are adaptive and instead are exposed to models who use more maladaptive problem-solving strategies, and, as a consequence, such youths may take on a stable coping response (e.g., negative learning attitude) which has deleterious behavioral correlates and adverse coping products (e.g., school failure and school leaving).

[15] Understanding youths' perceptions and reactive coping methods to experiences such as having a parent with a drug problem, living with parental rancor and divorce, becoming involved with or being exposed to drugs or alcohol, attending schools that are alienating, and having increased conflict with parents are all chronic, context-linked stresses that require reactive coping methods. The relationship between stressful events and adaptive corrective problem strategies (e.g., general positive attitude) deserves further inquiry. Furthermore, PVEST suggests a reciprocal relationship between perceptions and attitudes.

[16] Specifically and consistent with a phenomenological analysis, our perceptions of how others perceive us can influence our expectations, responsive attitudes and behaviors. This is complicated by the fact that our attitude and behaviors can influence how others perceive, respond, and react to us. Therefore, in considering the meaning of the findings from this study, it is important to keep in mind that this study focused on cognitive variables concerned with perceptions and attitudes. Except for a report of stressful events experienced in the past year, no behavioral variables were included that would indicate whether negative peer perceptions were, in fact, unfounded or not for any given student. Nevertheless, PVEST suggests that perceptions are important as a source of stress and can influence behavior even when they are not based necessarily "in fact." Therefore, if lack of acceptance or positive perception by teachers in the school context leads to youths' disfranchisement from the schooling process, the focus of students' perceptual processes may represent an important and necessary focal point for intervention efforts.

[17] As an intervention strategy to address adolescent problems, there has been significant national interest in the supportive role of mentoring. Our findings indicate that, particularly for males, youths' perceptions of teachers are critically important as a source of stress. The predictive pattern for males suggests the need for adult role models and supportive adults in the lives of youth who provide models of adaptive corrective problem-solving strategies (e.g., general positive attitude). Furthermore, interventions that focus on either perceived or real peer relations suggest other potentially important

pathways for enhancing youths' school engagement through the internalization of a less negative learning attitude.

[18] There was partial support for the second hypothesis which suggested that perceived positive teacher expectations for males and perceived unpopularity with peers would be the most important contributors to negative learning attitude. Table 3 indicated that the largest contributor was perceived unpopularity with peers; although, equally salient was perceived popularity with peers. Positive teacher perceptions was modestly significant for boys. On the other hand, for girls, only perceived unpopularity with peers significantly and consistently predicted negative learning attitude. The finding that perceived unpopularity with peers, for girls, represents the single significant predictor of negative learning attitude is consistent with other research demonstrating that female peer groups are especially important and different from male peer groups. As suggested, across the life course, social relationships appear to be unusually salient for health: physical and mental. The centrality and salience of the peer group for girls is important for programs of health promotion and enhancement. However, for males, the findings suggest additional and multiple roots of support and intervention: teacher supports, training programs and mentors as models of more adaptive corrective problem solving strategies (i.e., reactive coping methods). These data do not indicate non-peer group potential resources for girls, however. Perhaps, for females, stressful events should be thought of more in terms of group as opposed to individual experiences. Furthermore, it may be the case that general positive attitude, for females, should be thought of in terms of how it could be influenced by peer relations.

[19] The finding for this model suggest that particularly and consistently for African-American urban male teens, particular stresses are important in the prediction of negative learning attitude: positive teacher expectancies for Black males, perceived unpopularity with peers, and perceived popularity with peers; the relationships are in the expected direction. The reactive (adaptive) coping method, general positive attitude, appears to be an effective adaptive response to perceived unavailability of social supports as the source of stress in the prediction of the stable coping response: negative learning attitude. Having a generally positive attitude matters in the prediction of negative learning attitudes. These findings suggest its role as a singularly important and independent contributor for males' negative learning attitudes after controlling for risk, stressful events, and diverse sources of social support. In general, it is not a new notion that teachers and peers *matter* in the lives of youth (Irvine, 1988; Cunningham 1994). However, analyses suggest that specifically

perceived unpopularity with peers matter most for boys and girls; particularly for females, however, perceived popularity with peers does not seem as salient as their perceived unpopularity. Clearly all social supports are of special importance for males.

[20] Overall, perceived social supports are critically important as a source of stress and are linked to cultural contexts amenable to intervention. As suggested, the predictive models may be helpful in the "fine tuning" of intervention methods that should result in better self-organizational outcomes and life course opportunity. As an interpretive device, the PVEST model provides an important framework for clarifying complex context-linked phenomena.

## ☆ THE ARGUMENT

Following a brief introduction to the logic of PVEST, this article moves into a more specific discussion of the relationship between environment, self-organization, and outcomes. The overall goal is to demonstrate to the reader that linkages between environmental factors, identity, and outcomes are interrelated. This argument is structured as follows:

1. Self-organization (identity) enables youth to adjust or "self-correct" across different social, institutional, and cultural contexts (paragraph 1).

2. However, self-organization is itself influenced by the individual's subjective and personal interpretations of experience, along with developmental changes, such as puberty (paragraph 2).

3. Youth coming of age in "hostile" environments (that is, those characterized by high levels of negative feedback) therefore self-organize in ways that reconcile negative feedback with a more affirming view of themselves (paragraph 3).

4. These self-organizing processes may produce adaptive (resilient) or maladaptive (pathological) responses, depending on a variety of factors (paragraph 3).

5. This article explores the relationship between environmental risk factors, how those factors are perceived and experienced by youth, and self-organization (paragraph 4).

6. Specifically, this article explores the hypothesis that a negative learning attitude—in essence, a devaluing of school—emerges when negative feedback is present and there is no appropriate coping method available (paragraph 5).

7. Survey data are analyzed to assess the strength of relationships between these constructs, and to determine the extent to which negative feedback and coping methods influence self-organization (paragraph 5).

While this chapter focuses on how findings are situated and explained, there are a few aspects of the argument itself that are worth noting. First, as with other works featured in this book, the argument opens with the case for why this research matters and then moves into how the study was designed to meet the needs of the research. Particularly worth noting is the relationship between the study's theoretical framework (PVEST) and its conceptual framework, which argues for the importance of studying how environmental risk factors and coping responses influence school-relevant developmental outcomes. As we argued in Chapter 1, the theoretical framework is nested within the conceptual framework.

Second, more than any other article featured in this book, "A Self-Organization Perspective in Context" attempts simultaneously to stand alone and to tie into a much larger (and longer) body of work. A major challenge for this study and the article that resulted from it was to carve out a smaller piece of the larger framework and then to provide enough context for the reader to understand what the former says about the latter. This is best illustrated by Figure 6.1, which highlights specific pieces of the PVEST framework, linking each to a specific construct or variable presented in the article. "In this paper, we decide to look at just a part of the theory . . . [that] looked at identity as the outcome," Spencer explained. Put another way, PVEST includes a starting point (environment), an ending point (life outcomes), a set of mediating processes or factors, and hypothesized relationships among all three. But every study built on PVEST did not address all of the relationships posited by the larger theoretical framework. Spencer explained in the interview:

Where you assign or designate placement of a construct in a theoretical framework like this very often depends upon the nature of your questioning of some particular phenomenon. It is critical to determine your current place in the question-asking process. Specifically, what is the burning interest that you seek to make some sense of at the moment?

Given the response, you then move in that direction, and through your stepwise research efforts, then seek to obtain a bit of clarity for that specific segment. Following that step, you then add another piece later on. Thus, a theory-driven and linked programmatic research tradition includes an implicit and critical acknowledgment that you can't do it all or answer all of the relevant questions at one time.

In the present study, what was a mediating process in the larger framework (identity) becomes an outcome of interest for the conceptual framework presented in the article. This makes the study, as presented, more focused and tightly aligned with the constructs measured by the survey instruments. It also allows Spencer and her colleagues to address specific questions related to how stress impacts students' choices and influences school success.

Finally, it is worth noting the use of language in this article and what it says about the intended audience for the work. In Chapter 2, we noted that every argument needs to have a starting point, and the location of that starting point depends largely on the intended audience for the work. From the language used, it is readily apparent that "A Self-Organizational Perspective in Context" is written for an academic audience that is familiar with the basic tenets of developmental psychology. As such, the conceptual framework is not focused on arguing that resilience is important—it is assumed that the audience already understands the concept of resilience and believes that it is important. Instead, the article focuses on understanding how resilience works. Similarly, it assumes an understanding of phenomenology and of identity processes that is firmly rooted in the field of psychology. In this article, no attempt is made to locate this perspective alongside those from other disciplines; the focus is on analyzing a set of relationships using the tools and epistemology of a particular field. Given the audience for the article, this approach is entirely appropriate—it conveys the necessary information about the particulars of the analysis while assuming that the reader will be able to make sense of those specifics within the larger discourse of the discipline.

## ☆ PRESENTING AND DISCUSSING FINDINGS

The discussion section of this article picks up where the literature review leaves off: explaining the significance of a negative learning attitude within the context of PVEST (paragraph 6). Specifically, Spencer and colleagues argue that negative learning attitudes lead to negative life outcomes such as dropping out of school or academic delinquency. This effectively establishes negative learning attitude as a proxy outcome, and ties the smaller, more focused analyses presented in the article to the larger PVEST framework. As such, the introduction both reminds the reader about why the topic of the study is important (because negative learning outcomes are associated with adverse life consequences) and makes an argument about its broader significance.

Having re-engaged the argument for the study, the authors briefly remind the reader of its methodology (paragraphs 7 and 8). This includes a brief summation of the data and the primary hypotheses that were explored: the relationship between general positive attitude and negative learning attitude and the relationship between teachers' expectations or perceived unpopularity with peers and negative learning attitude. In three brief paragraphs, the authors have reminded the reader of the overall conceptual framework for the study and in doing so have set the stage for the discussion of findings that follows. There is an important lesson in this bit of setup work, especially for those employing quantitative methods. When presenting your findings, it is important to remember that on their own, the numbers are meaningless. Having worked with them extensively over a long period of time, it may be self-evident to you what they refer to, but not so evident to your reader. The values you report need to be attached to concepts, relationships, and, ultimately, your research questions.

With regard to the findings themselves, the discussion section actually tells two quite different stories about the relationship between findings and conceptual frameworks. The first offers a good example of what happens when researchers' findings more or less conform to their expectations: the results are used primarily to extend and support the conceptual framework. The second is just the opposite: a story of a finding that not only fails to conform to the researchers' expectations but also raises questions about the assumptions that led to those expectations in the first place. While these stories are somewhat intertwined within the article itself, we choose to discuss them separately here. Together, they offer a useful illustration of one of the tensions endemic to research: how you teach others about your work on the one hand, and how you yourself learn from it on the other.

## USING FINDINGS TO CONTEXTUALIZE ☆ AND EXTEND THE ARGUMENT

Many of the results presented in the article are consistent with the PVEST framework. The authors note that it is not surprising that female headship alone would not predict negative learning attitude (paragraph 9). It is not the fact of female headship that influences self-organization, they argue, but rather how female headship is experienced and interpreted that would likely have the greatest influence on coping responses and ultimately on self-organization. This is where the phenomenological perspective is emphasized—development is not viewed merely as a set of observable experiences or behaviors, but rather as the cumulative interpretation and integration of those experiences into a sense of self. The fact that female headship was not significant is therefore presented as evidence in support of this phenomenological perspective. "What we're saying," Spencer explained to us, "is that of all of the findings, this is one of the most important. Identity or the self-organizing process is critical, not the assumptions imposed concerning the salience of single headship. That is what is really key here."

As hypothesized (paragraph 5), there was an inverse relationship between having a general positive attitude (a reactive coping method) and a negative learning attitude (an emergent identity). The authors note that this finding is consistent with PVEST and then attempt to explain its implications (paragraph

12). They venture beyond specific findings to offer a possible explanation for why, given environmental stressors, some youth develop a general positive attitude while others do not. This entails an inversion of the relationship between the theoretical framework and the findings. The authors begin by noting that the findings validate PVEST, but then use PVEST to offer a hypothesis as to why general positive attitudes vary. Specifically, they suggest that youth may have differential exposure to others who are engaged in either adaptive or maladaptive coping responses, and that this exposure likely influences their own attitudes. This is consistent with the idea, central to PVEST, that individuals' processes for making sense of their experience are intersubjective. It also builds on an empirical finding from the study: that peer influences are important in shaping youths' stable coping responses. In sum, the conceptual framework for the article serves not only to contextualize empirical findings, but to offer reasoned explanations for those findings that extend beyond the analyses conducted.

Perceived social supports were also related to negative learning attitude in ways anticipated by PVEST. The strongest relationship was between perceived unpopularity with peers and a more negative learning attitude; for girls it was actually the *only* significant predictor. This finding warrants explanation on two levels. The first level relates to the implications and significance of perceived unpopularity (or popularity) with peers as a predictor of negative learning attitude (paragraph 14). As with the finding regarding a general positive attitude, the authors begin by noting that these findings are consistent with their original hypotheses (paragraph 5) and argue that they validate the importance of perceptions (the phenomenological perspective) when analyzing the relationship of environmental factors and developmental outcomes. They then argue that further attention to students' perceptual processes is warranted from a research perspective, and that efforts to strengthen students' peer relationships should be more of a focus from an intervention standpoint (paragraph 15). Again, this represents an extension of the argument from findings to implications.

The second level concerns the apparent differences between boys and girls with regard to other social support variables: perceived popularity with peers and perceived positive teacher expectations for black males. Here the authors attempt to explain why gender differences were evident (paragraph 9), arguing that research on how males and females experience stress suggests that the males do so in broad, undifferentiated ways (that is, stress is perceived as generalized and cumulative), while for females stress is more specific to particular sources. Further, they note, females are more likely than males to attempt to cope with stress through the formation of same-sex peer relationships. This explanation offers a good example of how additional literature (in this case from health research) can be integrated into a conceptual framework to help explain and contextualize specific findings.

In attempting to respond to a question that emerged from their research but was not directly answered by it, the authors address an important question faced by many researchers when presenting and contextualizing findings: how much do we need to explain, and how do we go about explaining it? It seems important that the results of this analysis differed for boys and girls. This is also consistent with the Ecological Systems Theory aspects of PVEST, in which social and cultural views and experiences of gender are clearly a factor in the process of self-organization. At a minimum, the authors would be justified in simply presenting these differences as evidence that such macro-level factors must be considered when studying development. But they go beyond that, introducing more general research on gender and the experience of stress in order to offer a possible explanation for the result they observed. It is important to note, however, that they do so with some caution. This is appropriate under the circumstances—the authors offer a reasoned interpretation of their finding, but are careful not to overstate the meaning of the finding itself.

In the conclusion (paragraphs 17 and 18), the authors note that while research literature has consistently documented that young people's relationships with both teachers and peers are important, findings from their analyses suggest that the importance of these relationships may be more differentiated and complex than originally thought, and that further investigation is warranted. They also note the potential implications for interventions, but only in the sense of general considerations. Like decisions about the starting point for one's argument, the nature of recommendations emerging from a study is a function of its intended audience. Because "A Self-Organizational Perspective in Context" is written for academics, it makes sense that its implications focus largely on conceptual and methodological implications for research.

In sum, the findings presented in this study are integrated with its conceptual framework in three ways. First, the authors respond directly to the research questions and hypotheses previously articulated. Second, they explain more broadly how the relationships evident in the data map onto PVEST, the study's theoretical framework. Finally, they indicate areas where further investigation into aspects of the framework is needed.

## LEARNING FROM SURPRISES: HOW FINDINGS ☆ RESHAPE CONCEPTUAL FRAMEWORKS

While many of the findings in "A Self-Organizational Perspective in Context" are consistent with PVEST and with the article's conceptual framework, one fairly significant result appears to contradict them. For boys, the experience of stressful events was strongly *positively* related to having a general positive attitude: the more stressful events reported, the more positive the general attitude. Similarly, the experience of stress was negatively related to a negative learning attitude: the more stress experienced, the *less* negative the learning attitude. The regression analysis yielded similar findings: the experience of stressful events was a significant predictor of less negative learning attitude, even when controlling for other factors.

As the authors note, PVEST would predict that experiencing more stress would be related to a less positive general attitude, and consequently a more negative learning attitude. In fact, the opposite relationship was found. They admit being surprised by this finding. But how they respond within the article itself is only part of the larger story. Equally important, this counterintuitive result led Spencer to reconsider some of her assumptions about the context in which stress is experienced, ultimately leading to significant changes in how PVEST is organized and presented.

In "A Self-Organizational Perspective in Context," Spencer and colleagues offer two tentative explanations for this result (paragraphs 10 and 12). First, they suggest that instead of signaling the presence of instability or negative feedback in boys' lives, reports of stressful events may in fact serve as an indication of *engagement* in schooling. As they assert, "youth may be heavily engaged in social activities which also result in significant opportunities for stressful events." Second, the authors posit that the relationship between stressful events and a general positive attitude may be bidirectional. Having a general positive attitude is not the result of experiencing stress, but rather a filter for interpreting those experiences. "To some extent," write the authors, "boys have learned to perceive certain experiences—that would be highly stressful and discouraging for others—as part of everyday existence" (p. 830).

Because the article was primarily focused on the relationship between social supports, coping methods, and self-organization, explaining this surprising finding was not the primary focus within the discussion section. The authors offer possibilities but do so only in brief, focusing instead on explaining the results that are more central to their hypotheses. But the importance of this surprise extends well beyond the article. The dissonance it created helped Spencer to rethink the relationship between environment, stress, and coping in ways that fundamentally changed PVEST. "The dilemma here is that we interpreted risk, in terms of stressful events, in a very simple way," she reflected in the interview. She continued:

> When considering stressful events, one could interpret them narrowly in terms of risk alone. That was not our intent. However, in fact, we did not include constructs and variables, which provided opportunities for other interpretations. For example, on the one hand, high-stress-experienced males may have interpreted or inferred more problem-solving competence as a consequence of having been burdened by significant levels of stress

and risk. Capturing that perspective would have been an important protective factor to capture in the conceptual framework. That is, representing PVEST as an exploration of human vulnerability—consistently representing both risk *and* protective factors—was critical. Thus, at the same time relative to the project's design, including both explicit protective factors and risks was key. Accordingly, their absence represented a clear oversight in the design of the published project and, thus, a lesson learned.

Accordingly, upon review, there were at least two problems with this conceptualization, Spencer explained. For one thing, young people experience different types of stress, with varying consequences. The measures used in the study failed to differentiate the possible perceptions of stressful experience, which may have been partly responsible for the finding. More important and as suggested, however, the analysis failed to account for protective factors, experienced in real time as supports, available to youth. The authors speculate in the article whether the experience of stressful events might actually be a proxy for such supports, but they had no way to explore that theory empirically. In subsequent work, however, Spencer has reframed both risk and stress in terms of *net vulnerability*, characterized by a combination of differentiated stress and the presence or absence of support. In later work (Spencer, 2006), she explains the concept as follows:

> Net vulnerability . . . consists of the contextual and personal characteristics that may potentially pose challenges during an individual's development. Risk contributors are factors that may predispose individuals to adverse outcomes. These may be offset by protective factors, thus defining net vulnerability for a given individual. (p. 642)

Spencer describes risk using a *dual-axis formulation*, essentially a two-by-two matrix with risk factors (*low, high*) on one side and protective factors (*low, high*) on the other. Using this more nuanced lens, Spencer offered a compelling critique of her earlier work:

> *Pointing to a diagram and referring to the high-risk and low-protective-factor versus the low-risk and high-protective-factor group, Spencer notes:* These are the two groups which obtain significant attention in the social sciences: Youth who are high risk with low protective factors, and kids who experience low risk and high protective factors. This latter group represents the unquestioned assumed standard of normal development and is usually comprised of white, middle-income, and, too often, male individuals. As noted, it has been the habit of social

science to compare these two groups. However, in using a dual-axis model to represent PVEST and its recognition of human vulnerability, we acknowledge the existence of a high-risk–high-support group as well as low-risk–low-support group of individuals who are generally ignored. However, for this particular publication, for the group of high-risk and high-stressed students, we failed to include measures designed to capture diverse types of support. In sum, we overlooked the need for inclusion of measures designed to account for the broad and varied sources of supports, that is, present and accessible even given the presence of high risk.

The evolution of PVEST offers an important lesson about the relationship between theoretical frameworks and empirical work. As we argued in Chapter 1, a theoretical framework is not simply applied to a setting—the data and findings are constantly reflecting and pushing back on the framework itself, offering valuable feedback about both its usefulness and conceptual soundness. Surprises are one of the ways in which this happens. (Null results are another.) For researchers, the important thing is to remain open to these opportunities to advance our learning and thinking. By definition, theoretical frameworks are complex (because they involve a fitting together of different theories) and acontextual (we develop and employ them to make sense of ambiguous situations or relationships). As we go through the process of systematically collecting and analyzing data related to those frameworks, we have more of an opportunity to examine them within the specific context we seek to learn about. From this perspective it becomes clear that theoretical frameworks are *supposed* to evolve.

## ☆ CONCLUSION

Throughout this book, we have sought to present academic argument as a series of sequenced, logical propositions, each building on the previous. We have defined the conceptual framework as an argument about the importance (reason) and quality (rigor) of a study or piece of writing. As we have shown in this chapter, the presentation and contextualization of findings serves two important functions related to the conceptual framework. First, it serves as an extension of the argument. If a conceptual framework is an argument about the worth of a question or questions, discussion of findings or results can be thought of as an argument about the significance of the answers to those questions. It takes the conceptual framework as a point of departure. Second, it provides a critical opportunity to reflect on and critique the conceptual framework. This applies to both the substantive assumptions and ideas that form the argument (in this chapter, for example, the relationship between stress and response) as well as the study's methodology (the degree to which risk is or is not differentiated). This critique is essential to good empirical research. Your conceptual framework, and the theories that fit within that framework, provide you with a reasonable rationale for your questions and methods. But that framework is also subject to what you learn from the data themselves. As such, findings are simultaneously an outgrowth of conceptual frameworks and feedback loop to strengthen and improve them.

## READING REFERENCES ☆

Chestang, L. W. (1972). *Character development in a hostile environment*. (Occasional Paper No. 3). Chicago: University of Chicago, School of Social Service Administration.

Cicchetti, D., Rogosch, F., Lynch, M., & Holt, K. (1993). Resilience in maltreated children: Processes leading to adaptive outcome. *Development and Psychopathology, 5*, 629–647.

Cicchetti, D., & Tucker, D. (1994). Development and self-regulatory structures of the mind. *Development and Psychopathology, 6,* 533–549.

Cunningham, M. (1994). *Expressions of manhood: Predictors of educational achievement and African-American adolescent males*. Unpublished doctoral dissertation, Emory University, Atlanta, GA.

Irvine, J. J. (1990). *Black students and school failure*. New York: Greenwood Press.

Lewis, M. (1995). Cognition-emotion feedback and the self-organization of developmental paths. *Human Development, 38*, 71–102.

Took, K. J., & Weiss, D. S. (1994). The relationship between heavy metal and rap music and adolescent turmoil: Real or artifact? *Adolescence, 29*(115), 613–621.

Wingard, D. L. (1987). *Social behavior and biological factors influencing the sex differential of longevity*. Background paper prepared for the National Institute on Aging, Washington, DC.

# CHAPTER 7

# THE CONCEPTUAL FRAMEWORK AS GUIDE AND BALLAST

As we established in Chapter 1, there is considerable confusion and even disagreement about both the content and role of conceptual frameworks in social science research. The ambiguity around the substance, form, and terminology of conceptual frameworks, we argued, leads to an array of terms—*theoretical framework*, *conceptual framework*, *conceptual model*, *theory*, and *literature review*—being used imprecisely or even interchangeably, as well as to amorphous expectations and directives for the conceptual framing of empirical research. Despite all of the attention given to the importance of conceptual framing in master's theses and doctoral dissertations and in academic research more broadly, many academics struggle to explain how such framing occurs, what a conceptual framework comprises, how it influences the research process, and why a conceptual framework is important to the processes and outcomes of empirical work. Throughout this book, we have argued that, without clarity as to the purposes and roles of a conceptual framework, it simply becomes one of many items on a researcher's to-do list rather than a significant, generative aspect of the research development process. Worse yet, because there is no focused emphasis on iterative conceptual development and refinement and its relationship to research design and implementation, research often remains undertheorized, weakly conceptualized, and less generative of quality data, data analysis, and findings than it should be. In this book we have endeavored to clarify the terminology, functions, roles, and uses of conceptual frameworks through the close examination of real-world research examples, illustrating how each is conceptualized, constructed, and implemented within and across the stages of the research process across disciplines, fields, and methodological approaches. Examining each of these four conceptual frameworks as they ground and guide the four research projects at the center of *Reason and Rigor* helps illustrate the active roles, uses, and creative value of a conceptual framework as well as its recursive and malleable state throughout the research process. One of our main points in this book is that the conceptual framework is influenced by, as it influences, the research process at all stages.

Throughout this book we have explored the complex and multidimensional role that conceptual frameworks play in shaping empirical research. We have defined a conceptual framework as an argument as to why the topic of a study is significant and why the theoretical and methodological tools for conducting the study are rigorous and appropriate. By *argument*, we mean that a conceptual framework is a series of sequenced, logical propositions aimed to convince readers of the importance and rigor of a study. By *appropriate and rigorous*, we mean that a conceptual framework should help the researcher to argue convincingly that (a) the research questions are an outgrowth of the argument for significance and relevance to the field or fields; (b) the data to be collected provide the researcher with the "raw material" necessary to explore and substantively respond to the guiding research questions and topic; and (c) the analytic approach will allow the researchers to effectively respond to the guiding research questions.

We have stated throughout *Reason and Rigor* that the conceptual framework is a guide for research; it serves to situate the research questions and the methods for exploring them within the broader context of existing knowledge about a topic even as the researcher seeks to generate new knowledge about that topic. As we stated in Chapter 1, carefully examining prior research is not simply a lofty academic exercise but is a vital process of learning from the experience and expertise of other experts in the field. A conceptual framework allows you, the researcher, to make informed, reasoned, and defensible choices about how to explore research topics and themes that are underexplored or to explore old questions in new contexts and with new theoretical frames. A conceptual framework matches your research questions with those choices and aligns your analytic tools and methods with your questions. It also guides the ways that you think about collecting, analyzing, describing, and interpreting your data. Further, a well-articulated conceptual framework helps you to conceptualize, theorize, and critically examine positionality in relation to your choice of research topics, approaches, and methods. It is for all of these reasons—the range and variation of crucial roles that a conceptual framework plays—that we view the conceptual framework as a guide and ballast for empirical studies. This range of roles is also why we strongly argue that a conceptual framework is different from—broader than—a theoretical framework. We have argued throughout this book that a theoretical framework—the way in which a researcher engages with, integrates, and argues from existing theories within and across relevant fields—is one piece of a broader conceptual framework that also incorporates personal interests and motivations as well as topical research that may not be explicitly theoretical. Further, your conceptual framework integrates the contexts, both historical and contemporary (for example, macrosocial and institutional), of the research questions and setting as well as the positionalities—individual, social, and institutional—that shape and influence the research as it is conceived and as it develops over time. In sum, the conceptual framework helps us to develop the conceptual tools we need to uncover, decipher, and interrogate the multiple, intersecting contexts of our research and to explore these contexts as points of inquiry throughout every stage of the research process.

The role that conceptual frameworks play in research is multifaceted and iterative; as this book suggests, an examination of these various roles helps us as researchers to make critical connections between the theoretical and methodological components of our research. A well-articulated conceptual framework helps us to clarify for ourselves and for others what is important to us as researchers about the questions or problems that emerge from our intellectual and practical engagement in the world broadly and in our research contexts specifically. There is great range and variation in the scale of why a study "matters," depending in part on the audience and contexts. Developing sound conceptual frameworks allows us as researchers to situate ourselves in terms of what is meaningful in the field or fields that form the context of our studies and questions. Additionally, one component of a conceptual framework is about our own intellectual curiosity, our personal and professional biographies and histories, and our macrosocial (sociopolitical) and microsocial (institutional) locations and positionalities. These aspects of our personal, social, and organizational identities have much to do with what we choose to study and how we choose to study it. In this sense, our personal interests and stories are a foundational part of our conceptual frameworks and therefore of our research as a whole. Our conceptual frameworks are informed by, as they inform, our ideological, theoretical, positional, and relational worlds. Conceptual frameworks allow for focused, systematic exploration of these aspects of who we are, what we study, why we choose to study it, and how we choose to study it. A well-conceived and -articulated conceptual framework allows for the deep conceptualization of linkages between these various aspects of our lives and our work; it guides us in our exploration of these crosscurrents in our approach to the research and throughout the implementation of the research itself.

Focusing on the work of four highly accomplished contemporary researchers—Frederick Erickson, Michelle Fine, James Spillane, and Margaret Beale Spencer—we have closely examined the ways in which each of these researchers' conceptual frameworks inform and shape different aspects and stages of the research process. While we have examined the relationship of the conceptual framework to various stages of the research process in each of our chapters, common across the examples included in the book is an emphasis on the conceptual framework as a pragmatic tool for uncovering and exploring (a) questions of relevance, applicability, and uses of empirical research; (b) the appropriateness of different types of research questions for specific topics, contexts, and methods; (c) the alignment of data collection and analysis to research questions; and (d) the interpretation and description of findings. In considering the role of conceptual frameworks in depth within each of these realms, our aim is to help you to conceptualize points of connection and integration between theories and methods. Each example in this book shows the direct implications of engaging in intentional and systematic ways in the development and ongoing refinement of one's conceptual framework. Looking across chapters illustrates the ways in which theory, empirical research, and multiple, intersecting layers of context shape and influence the conceptual framework as that framework guides and grounds the research process. This recursive process of conceptual framework development and research development and ongoing refinement reflects the iterative nature of empirical research. It is, at its methodological ideal, a deeply recursive and dynamic process of meaning making and intellectual engagement.

In Chapter 3, "Excavating Questions: Conceptual Frameworks and Research Design," which focused on the work of James Spillane, we explored the ways that the development of Spillane's conceptual framework influenced his choices about research design. This chapter helps us to understand the role of the conceptual framework in defining, justifying, and contextualizing research questions and in guiding key decisions about the types of data required to explore and respond to those questions. Spillane's research helps us to examine how choices made about the conceptual framework of a study shape research design and significantly influence data collection and analysis. Exploring his work through this lens helps us to understand the interrelated and evolving nature of conceptual frameworks and research design. As we stated in the chapter, "Local Theories of Teacher Change" (the focal study analyzed in Chapter 3) uses the findings from a prior study that Spillane conducted to develop and contextualize a new set of research questions, and while it works from an earlier data set, it employs a new analytic approach—a shift from an inductive approach to a deductive one in the collection and analysis of his data—that is an outgrowth of modifications and refinements in the conceptual framework. That shift was precipitated by the incorporation of a new theoretical framework into his larger conceptual framework. Chapter 3 helps us to understand that as a result of the close link between conceptual frameworks and research design, development in one leads to development in the other. As we saw in that chapter, the implications of this engagement with his conceptual framework led Spillane to make significant, formative changes in his data analysis, which then led to a different, innovative set of findings and assertions back in the field.

In Chapter 4, "The Role of the Conceptual Framework in Data Collection and Fieldwork," we used the work of Michelle Fine to focus on the iterative, recursive nature of conceptual frameworks as they are developed, challenged, and refuted through reflexive engagement in research fieldwork. This chapter explored the layered and powerful influence of conceptual frameworks on data collection and fieldwork choices. As Fine's work shows, conceptual frameworks are simultaneously guides for and products of an iterative, ever-evolving process of development that happens through critical dialogue and engagement in the research as well as the researcher's reflexive engagement with her own meaning-making processes as she engages in fieldwork. In Fine's work we are able to see, because she makes it transparent, how these meaning-making processes challenge and refute as well as support and uphold specific theoretical and ideological influences on the research. We argue that it is precisely through reckoning with the tensions and crosscurrents that arise when you scrutinize the influences—relational, positional, ideological, political, social, national, and transactional—on your research that the most creative, elucidating research findings emerge. Fine's work offers an excellent example of the close, nonlinear relationship between who you are, what you study, and how you study it. As we have argued throughout the book, a conceptual framework is the embodiment of all three. As a researcher, you make choices throughout the research process about what you think is important and interesting, and these choices reflect who you are as a person and what you value as a researcher. They also reflect where and with whom you work. The language you use to describe the research, the methods you employ, and how you write up and present findings are all a function of the social, political, and professional worlds you inhabit as a scholar. Fine's work elucidates that powerfully and stands as a poignant example of the role of conceptual frameworks for examining and thinking through issues of positionality, the relational nature of research and how these are influenced by large-scale and small-scale sociopolitical forces and realities.

In Chapter 5, "Conceptual Frameworks and the Analysis of Data," we turned to the work of Frederick Erickson. Based on Erickson's research process, we argued that at its ideal, a conceptual framework informs data analysis in direct, meaningful, and, ideally, transparent ways. We drew lessons from Erickson's example about how a well-articulated conceptual framework helps a researcher to (a) make decisions about what is most important to pay attention to and substantively focus on throughout the analytic process; (b) choose appropriate tools for organizing and filtering the data; (c) make informed choices about taking an inductive or a deductive approach to data analysis; and (d) justify and make visible his own interpretive processes and choices, which are themselves shaped by his interests, values, and background. In particular, we highlight how the central constructs or areas of focus identified within a conceptual framework—the timing of interaction, in this instance—are operationalized in the analysis of data.

"Going for the Zone," the empirical work at the heart of Chapter 5, is a particularly compelling example of the role of a conceptual framework in data analysis because it shows how the researcher draws upon, as he enters into dialogue with, multiple intersecting fields that contextualize and frame the research questions and context in focus. Erickson's engagement in multiple fields—sociolinguistics, discourse analysis, neo-Vygotskianism, social interaction theory, music theory, teacher research, and theories of culture and communication broadly—spans four decades and becomes instantiated in an interdisciplinary approach to making sense of data that were analyzed earlier using different theoretical frames. Erickson's own learning on the topic of student-teacher interaction in classroom contexts builds on (as it adds to) generations of field development and influences his approach to analyzing pre-existing data with a new and different focus. His long-standing engagement in iterative and reflexive framework development illustrates the ways in which analysis is a conceptually embedded process that can shift and change as one's theoretical lenses and conceptual framing shift over time. Erickson's consideration of a new theoretical framework led him to view, or review, the data differently, to see new and different things in them, and to recast his argument in an innovative direction. This can teach us a great deal about how conceptual frameworks inform analytic themes or categories as well as about how working theoretical frames influence quite specific moments of data reduction, organization, and analysis. As Chapter 5 presents, data analysis and theory development are, ideally, in an iterative and dynamic relationship.

In Chapter 6, "Expanding the Conversation, Extending the Argument: The Role of Conceptual Frameworks in Presenting, Explaining, and Contextualizing Findings," we focused on the work of Margaret Beale Spencer to discuss how researchers use conceptual frameworks to contextualize and make sense of findings as well as how findings are used to review, revise, and, ultimately, strengthen one's conceptual framework. The study by Spencer and her colleagues shows what can happen when you encounter surprises in your data, and how you can learn from those discoveries. The evolution of the Phenomenological Variant of Ecological Systems Theory (described in Chapter 6) offers an important lesson about the relationship between theoretical frameworks and empirical work. As we argued in Chapter 1, a theoretical framework is not simply applied to a setting—the data and findings constantly reflect and push back on the framework itself, offering valuable feedback about both its utility and its conceptual strength. As we see in Spencer's case, it is crucial to remain open to these discoveries so that you can develop your understanding of your topic and questions. From this perspective it becomes clear that theoretical (and conceptual) frameworks are *supposed* to evolve, and that you must be attuned to shifts and changes as they emerge. We see in Spencer's work that the presentation and contextualization of findings serves two important functions related to the conceptual framework. First, it extends the argument. If a conceptual framework is an argument about the value of our research questions, discussion of findings can be thought of as an argument about the significance of the answers to those questions, taking the conceptual framework as a point of departure. Second, it provides a vital opportunity to reflect on and engage in data-based critique of the conceptual framework. This applies to both the substantive assumptions and ideas that form the argument (in this chapter, for example, the relationship between stress and response) as well as the methodological approach employed in the study. In this sense, findings are an outgrowth of conceptual frameworks and a response that strengthens and improves upon them.

Within and across these four empirical studies, we see that the conceptual framework is more than a passive artifact or academic hoop to jump through and more than a static graphic of literatures read or key concepts in a vacuum. Rather, it is a dynamic meeting place of theory and method; it charts and provides a structure in which to analyze, over time, the multifaceted, layered, and complicated influences on one's research in all of its messiness and complexity. A well-articulated conceptual framework instantiates itself deeply in empirical work, and serves to guide, ground, and challenge us and our work as we reflexively engage in developing and refining it. In order for your conceptual frameworks to serve these purposes, however, you must be committed to engaging in a systematic and reflective approach to the development, construction, and enactment of your research. In this sense, the conceptual framework forces you to be intentional in your work in a manner that is both generative of and generated by your research. While the four scholars whose work is featured in this book are vastly different in terms of their research interests, disciplines and fields, methodological approaches, and the degree to which they explicitly address issues of ideology and positionality in their research, all four engage in this type of sustained reflection, critique, and, ultimately, revision of their conceptual frameworks. Their work offers powerful examples of how conceptual frameworks provide a milieu for you to clarify, first for yourself and then for your audiences, the specific conceptual terrain upon which you build your study. To extend the metaphor, a solid conceptual framework helps you chart your expedition through theoretical, contextual, and conceptual terrain with increased clarity, depth of insight, and transparency. It helps you to cultivate your tools of conceptualization, articulation, and exploration of critical connections and integrations within and across fields, topics, and emerging understandings more broadly.

Throughout *Reason and Rigor* we have looked deeply into the roles, uses, and applications of conceptual frameworks. In each chapter and across the chapters, our goal is to develop an understanding of the functional role conceptual frameworks play in organizing and guiding empirical research. A conceptual framework helps you to figure out how to engage deeply with existing knowledge in conjunction with your own interests and observations, and therefore to ask better questions, develop robust and justifiable strategies for exploring these questions, and explain both the value and limitations of your findings. Conceptual frameworks are necessary for developing and planning a study and, as well, help you deal with and address complexity in terms of questions and problems, ambiguity in terms of which fields relate to the topic and how, as well as to respond to changes in the fields your work inhabits, because those fields are not static. We have argued in this book that a well-articulated conceptual framework helps you to reason through and make sense of the intellectual, cultural, and institutional milieu of your work as well as the arguments you construct in your research within these realms. Our goal in the next section is to provide some useful questions and structures that can inform and guide you through various thought experiments and exercises that will help you think about your conceptual framework and its relationship to your study.

## ☆ DEVELOPING A CONCEPTUAL FRAMEWORK

As the preceding chapters show, every conceptual framework has its own story. Together, the four stories presented in this book offer a number of useful lessons about how to develop, use, and refine a conceptual framework.

What we offer below is not a how-to guide. Just as there is no single, best format for making an argument, so there is no single "right" way to build a conceptual framework. Indeed, one of the overarching themes of this book has been the role of the researcher's judgment in making decisions in ambiguous circumstances: How does who I am—as an individual whose history, perspectives, decisions, and experiences are shaped within large-scale sociopolitical forces—affect what I study? Where and when do I engage in fieldwork? What kinds of data do I need in order to answer my guiding research questions? How will I know when I have enough data? How do I know when to revisit or reconsider my theoretical framework or to introduce new theoretical perspectives in my analysis? Each of these questions appears in the preceding chapters. In each case, the researcher had to make a reasoned, principled choice about how to answer each question as it arose. And in each instance, the conceptual framework for the study helped to anchor their considerations.

In the remainder of this chapter, we combine lessons from the four scholars featured in this book with those from our own experiences and the experiences of our students to offer readers guidelines for developing and using conceptual frameworks. We first highlight several overarching themes that appear across chapters: the personal and autobiographical nature of conceptual frameworks, the role of conceptual frameworks in making and changing research plans, and the process of simultaneously being open to and pushing back on existing theory. We then offer suggestions about how to develop and refine your own conceptual framework. We think of this process as one of *reflexive engagement*—thinking iteratively about the connections between our own interests and values, what we are learning in the field and from our data, and what that tells us about the topic or phenomenon we are trying to understand. While this term reflects language more frequently employed in qualitative methods, we hope that by this point it has become clear that mixed methods and quantitative researchers often engage in a similar type of reflective thinking and analysis. And that reflexive engagement is an important, generative, and valuable approach to research within and across methodological approaches.

## STARTING POINTS: SELF AND AUDIENCE ☆

As each of the chapters in this book shows, there are really two ways of thinking about the starting point for a conceptual framework. The first is a careful consideration of where and how you began to think about what you want to study. One of the more striking aspects of the four research stories told in this book is how frequently and powerfully autobiographical the origins of research can be. In telling us about the origins of their research interests, three of the four scholars featured told us stories about their childhoods and their families. These stories remind us that however technical and complex the work of research becomes, it is also fundamentally human. The larger point here is not that all research needs to be deeply and personally meaningful. Curiosity, interest, and a sense of what types of research are needed are all perfectly reasonable rationales for selecting a particular topic or question. What is needed, however—and this is especially true for dissertation work, which can be an endurance test—is a critically conceptualized and carefully articulated personal connection to the work. Knowing what you want to study is obviously the starting point for conceptual frameworks and research in general, but being aware of why you, personally, want to study it is equally important. Engaging in this discovery process can help you as a researcher to develop a working sense of your own intuitions and motivations as well as the assumptions or biases you may be bringing to the work. This book is built upon several perspectives on empirical research, among them that (1) research is not neutral or apolitical; it does not happen in a vacuum, but rather, it is directly shaped and influenced by sets of broader contexts ranging from the personal to the political, social, and institutional; (2) there are most often autobiographical motivations for research, be they personal, professional, or some combination thereof; and (3) all researchers (indeed all human beings) are informed by personal biases, presuppositions, and assumptions, and these must be carefully uncovered and critically engaged with in order for research to be as authentic and trustworthy as possible (Nakkula & Ravitch, 1998). As we have stated throughout the book, we see developing and refining a conceptual framework as an ongoing process of critically examining and reckoning with these forces and their influence on our empirical work.

The second "point of departure" is where you ask your reader to begin, and that is largely a question of audience. All four of the empirical studies discussed in this book assume something about the reader: what they know or do not know, or what interests they might bring to the text. Because each of the works presented here was published in an academic journal or as a chapter in an edited volume, all assume that their typical reader is academically oriented and likely somewhat familiar with and interested in their field. For example, Spillane does not try to convince his readers that education policy is important, nor does Spencer feel the need to argue that low-income African American boys are often exposed to risk. More subtly, at least two of the articles anticipate a certain political orientation from their readership. Neither Fine nor Spencer spend much time trying to convince the reader that academic work has traditionally aided in the misrepresentation (at best) and oppression (at worst) of marginalized populations. They assume that this is largely understood, and instead begin by explaining to the reader how they engage with and counter that dynamic in their work.

## MAKING—AND BREAKING—YOUR PLANS ☆

Each of the four conceptual frameworks presented in this book clearly shows how the framing of arguments about what to study has significant implications for the design and execution of empirical research by highlighting how this works for a specific phase of the research process. But an equally important point is made across all four chapters: research is dynamic, not static. The more expert we become in a topic, the more nuanced our view becomes, and the more we expose ourselves to observations or findings that challenge and raise questions about our original assumptions. For example, Fine's expanding understanding of the significance of "the hyphen" as both metaphor and method reflects this natural progression, as does Spillane's convergence on theories of learning as central to understanding local implementation of state reforms. Additionally, because the conceptual work of research unfolds over time, there is always the possibility that the work of others shapes our own. All four of the scholars featured in this book told stories about how their peers, colleagues, and mentors shaped and reshaped their thinking over time. Erickson, for example, recounted how conversations with friend and colleague Ray McDermott led him to see what was happening in his data through a lens that more explicitly focused on power and influence. Finally, just as our thinking changes as our research unfolds, so do our understandings of the physical context in which the research is conducted. This has profound implications for the data we collect, even if our instruments or procedures for collecting it remain unchanged. In each of these four cases, changes in thinking about the researcher's topic or the context of the research precipitated changes in methods. For Spillane, it precipitated a shift to a deductive analytic process using a new theoretical framework. For Fine, it meant shifting into more mixed methods work and involving participants more fully in the research design and development process. For Erickson, it gave rise to an innovative concept, the relational concept of "turn sharks," and a different way of analyzing timing in interactions. These types of shifts are a natural, and often desirable, part of the research process. A good conceptual framework provides a clearly articulated reference point from which we can observe, and make sense of, these changes as they unfold.

## ☆ THE CONVERSATION: FROM LISTENING TO SPEAKING

In each of the works discussed in this book, we (and the authors themselves) show how previous research and theory shaped their thinking about what to study and how to study it. Once these researchers established their own starting points (as described above) they opened themselves up to be influenced by others. This is evident in the way Spencer defines identity, perceptions of experience, self-organization, and risk. It appears in Erickson's invocation of neo-Vygotskian theory, and in Spillane's extension of the arguments of Deborah Ball and David Cohen. It also emerges in the stories these four scholars told us during their interviews about their own learning; each could readily recite their intellectual autobiography, recounting changes in their own thinking as they engaged with different bodies of theory and research as well as in dialogue with others.

As Maxwell (2009) and Dressman (2008) point out, however, the relationship of research to theory is not unidirectional. Just as theory shapes our work (and our thinking about doing the work), what we learn through research leads us to revisit and reconsider established theory. As researchers, our job is not only to draw on theory but also to engage with and critique it. It is significant, then, that Spencer's research not only builds on theories of identity but also critiques their lack of reference to social context and power, and that her findings about links between risk exposure and attitudes led her to significantly revise her own theoretical framework; or in the case of Erickson, that looking at his data through a neo-Vygotskian lens led him to interrogate what he viewed as the interactional naïveté of existing theories.

In Chapter 2, we highlight the question of when and how to enter "the conversation already happening" as represented by academic literature. The four examples presented in this book suggest that the answer may be far from simple. On the one hand, you make an initial foray into the conversation when you justify the study. This constitutes a first full articulation of your conceptual framework. But to continue the metaphor, you should not simply enter the conversation and then withdraw. Rather, it is vital to remain fully engaged, interjecting your voice where you see it as needed or appropriate. Further, what you choose to add to the conversation may be quite different at the end of your study than it was at the beginning. It is important to engage in this process as a critical, active interlocutor rather than a passive, disengaged consumer of others' work. Working to develop and articulate your conceptual framework can be thought of as a way to engage in meaningful dialogue with other thinkers; it can and should be a structure that encourages and supports critical, integrative sense making that is connected to the work of others. What follows are examples of specific approaches to engaging in this multilayered process.

## STRATEGIES AND EXERCISES FOR ☆ DEVELOPING CONCEPTUAL FRAMEWORKS

Reflexive engagement requires that you create structures in which you can, from the outset of the research development process and incrementally over time, examine your own assumptions and motivations for studying a particular topic in a specific context, to ask broader questions about where the field is in terms of what you think of as "the conversations already happening," and to examine the relationships of research questions and methodological approach. In the discussion that follows, we offer strategies to assist in cultivating and sustaining a reflexively engaged approach throughout the research process, including the development of prompted research exercises, concept maps, research memos, and maintaining a research journal. The ideas below are intended to sketch out possibilities for structured thought experiments; they are not meant to be exhaustive or prescriptive. We strongly encourage you to engage in these exercises individually as well as in dialogue and collaboration with others who will engage thoughtfully and critically with you as you design and carry out your research, pushing you to examine parts of yourself and your research that you might otherwise take for granted or leave unexamined. Dialogue and exchange are essential to the trustworthiness of your empirical work, and we strongly encourage an approach to research that is dialogical and relational as well as internally engaged. The two go hand in hand as means of conducting the most rigorous, credible research possible. Conceptualizing and carefully documenting these processes is an important part of your methodological approach.

It is important to engage wholeheartedly in the asking of questions—sometimes sequentially and sometimes iteratively—about what is of value to you as a researcher and why it is valuable, useful, and important. What follows are broad areas for examination and reflection, with sets of possible questions to explore in each realm (though we would argue that these areas bleed into each other and should not necessarily be compartmentalized). We offer this as a list of guiding points of inquiry but not as a proscriptive or limiting set of questions. Ideally, you would return to specific questions at various stages throughout the research process.

## ☆ IDENTIFYING YOUR INTERESTS, BELIEFS, AND MOTIVATIONS FOR DOING RESEARCH

The following are questions that we encourage you to explore in order to engage in a process of self-examination at the outset of your research and then iteratively throughout the research process.

- What is interesting to me and why?
- What personal and professional motivations do I have for engaging in this research? How might these motivations influence how I think about and approach the topic?
- What are my beliefs about the people, places, and ideas involved in and related to my study? Where do these beliefs come from?
- What orientations to the topic, setting, and concepts do I have? Where do these ideas come from?
- What is my sense of the relationship between the large-scale and small-scale sociopolitical circumstances in which people make meaning and choices in their lives? With respect to the participants in my study specifically?
- What is my "agenda" for taking up this topic in this setting at this time? (*Note:* Having and agenda is not necessarily a bad thing. This may be the foundation of your argument!) What influences this agenda?
- How might my guiding agenda contribute, both positively and negatively, to my research design? Implementation? Analysis? Findings?
- What hunches do I have about what I might find and discover? What informs these hunches?
- What concerns, hopes, and expectations do I have for this research?
- What aspects, if any, of this research are autobiographically motivated? How, and in what ways? How might this impact my research?
- Why am I doing this research at this time—of my career, in history, within this setting? How might this historical moment influence various aspects of the research design and process?

## ☆ EXAMINATION OF THE "CONVERSATIONS ALREADY HAPPENING"

The following questions relate to how your proposed research fits into the landscape of what is already known about that topic, phenomenon, and population.

- What are the major conversations in the field or fields that form the context for my research topic and questions?
- What are some of the major arguments and positions in these fields?
- What do I think about the various strands of these conversations?
- What is the next critical set of questions to ask within these fields?
- Is the next set of questions about theory testing? Is it to contribute to a field or fields by studying something already researched with new methods or in a new setting?
- Which fields and disciplines intersect in ways that contextualize and frame my questions or topic?
- What are the major tensions and disagreements within and across these fields? What is my critique of these various overlaps, tensions, and disagreements?
- What do I hope to contribute to these conversations?
- How do I intend to include these various conversations in my examination of the existing literature?
- What are my thoughts and concerns about how these fields have constructed the issues at hand?
- Are there voices or points of view left out of or marginalized within these conversations? If so, who is left out and why might that be the case? And how might that influence my own construction of this topic or my research questions?
- How do I conceptualize and position my research in relation to the conversations already happening? And why am I making these choices?
- Looking within and across fields and disciplines, what are some of the differences in how these topics and questions are framed? How do I relate that to my own thinking?
- What methodological approaches do various researchers in these fields use in their research? Why? How do these approaches relate to my own methodological choices?
- What are the methodological strengths or weaknesses of the work that has already been done? How have methodological trends influenced what is known about this topic?

## ONGOING QUESTIONS AND CONCERNS ☆ ABOUT THE RESEARCH

The following questions can be asked throughout the process of engaging in research fieldwork. In essence, these are ways of "checking in" with aspects of your conceptual framework throughout the process of data collection and analysis.

- What do I tend to gravitate to in my observations and interpretations, and why? What can I learn from this about my approach to research?
- To what extent are these proclivities informed by my conceptual framework? To what extent do they help me cultivate a better sense of influences on my thinking, both broadly and specifically in the field?
- What emerging hypotheses or hunches do I notice? How might I theorize these in relation to the literature? In relation to my data?
- Is my conceptual framework limiting or shading my view of my setting, participants, or data? (Again, this is not necessarily a bad thing, but it is important to be aware of.) If so, in what ways?
- What am I learning during my fieldwork, and am I problematizing my learning as I go? In what ways? How might I endeavor to do so more fully?
- What assumptions am I making about local meaning making and knowledge? To what extent might these differ from my own interpretations as a researcher?
- What biases might I have in relation to local meaning making and knowledge? How can I best interrogate my assumptions as I move through the research process?
- How does what I am learning from my data inform or push back on elements of my conceptual framework? On existing conceptualizations of the phenomena under study?
- To what extent are the assumptions I made in the design phase about what was important or relevant to my study supported by my data? What blind spots might I have overlooked?
- What alternative interpretations or explanations exist for what I see in the data?
- What other kinds of data might I need to be able to more fully respond to my research questions?
- What issues of validity or trustworthiness are emerging, and how am I engaging with and addressing them?
- How does my identity and positionality—psychological, social, and institutional—influence the research process? And how can I address the aspects of this that need to be attended to?
- What disconfirming evidence can I find that challenges my existing understanding and interpretation of the data?
- What are alternative interpretations of the data? How can I seek those out as a part of the research process?

These types of questions, if asked in ongoing and systematic ways, help lead us as researchers to critically reflect on and gain insight into the motivations for and the findings of our empirical work. This reflexive process is in part about engaging in ongoing reflection and in part about challenging one-self to stay tuned into the research on multiple levels as it develops. Again, we urge researchers not only to engage in this kind of structured, prompted reflection in writing (since writing engenders a focused commitment to examination and critical inquiry), but also to engage in dialogue with col-leagues or peers who will challenge them to examine these issues in layered, complex, constructively critical ways (Leshem, 2007). Complicating our research in these ways is essential to its reliability and constructive develop-ment. What follows are some written structures and processes that can assist researchers in engaging in focused, critical, systematic sense making in relation to their empirical research.

## CONCEPT MAPS ☆

Concept maps have been around for decades. There are a number of valu-able texts that offer suggestions for concept mapping broadly and the visual representation of conceptual frameworks specifically. These texts have a variety of definitions of conceptual frameworks (as reviewed in Chapter 1) and approach the creation and development of conceptual frameworks and concept mapping from a variety of vantage points. Shared across them is the idea of visually mapping the various components of your conceptual frame-work as a means to clarifying connections between the various conceptual, contextual, and theoretical influences on a research study. Two of the most popular books that provide both novice and experienced researchers with tools for developing conceptual frameworks, as mentioned earlier, are Maxwell (2005) and Miles and Huberman (1994). Maxwell defines concept maps in this way:

> A concept map of a theory is a visual display of that theory—a picture of what the theory says is going on with the phenomenon you're studying. These maps do not depict the study itself, nor are they a specific part of either a research design or a proposal. . . . Rather, concept mapping is a tool for developing the conceptual framework for your design. . . . A concept map consists of two things: concepts and the relationships among these. (p. 47)

Maxwell (2005) asserts that the two main reasons, as he sees them, for developing concept maps are (1) "[to] pull together, and make visible, what your implicit theory is, or to clarify an existing theory"; and (2) "to *develop* theory. . . . [Concept maps] can help you see unexpected connections or identify holes or contradictions in your theory and help you to figure out ways to resolve these" (p. 47). He argues that concept maps require an iterative development process, and his book offers several structured exercises that can help researchers develop concept maps that are fitting and useful for their studies.

Miles and Huberman (1994) suggest that conceptual frameworks can be developed as both graphic representations and narratives, and suggest that concept maps are a critical tool in the development of a conceptual framework. They assert that concept maps are best developed graphically rather than in narrative form because that allows the researcher to visually lay out sets of relationships to explore and make sense of. Miles and Huberman assert that mapping concepts is foundational to solid working theories in empirical work:

> As qualitative researchers collect data, they revise their frameworks—make them more precise, replace empirically feeble bins with more meaningful ones, and reconstrue relationships. Conceptual frameworks are simply the current version of the researcher's map of the territory being investigated. As the explorer's knowledge of the terrain improves, the map becomes correspondingly more differentiated and integrated. (p. 20)

While Miles and Huberman (1994) speak directly to qualitative researchers, we have argued throughout this book that the development of conceptual frameworks is a critical process for researchers using qualitative, quantitative, and mixed methods approaches. Whether your work is qualitative, quantitative, or mixed, mapping relevant central concepts visually can help to refine your working understandings of the topics and contexts at play in your research by forcing you to represent relationships visually as well as in narrative form. For example, in Chapter 6, we include an example of a concept map in an excerpt from Spencer's chapter "A Phenomenological Variant of Ecological Systems Theory." This concept map is integrated into the text as a figure (Figure 6.1) and is titled "Model of relationship among female, headship, stressful events, perceived social supports, general positive attitude, and learning attitude" (page 116). In addition to illustrating hypothesized relationships between various factors, the figure also illustrates the relevant constructs employed in data collection and analysis and implies particular analytic approaches focused on the strength of those relationships.

This particular concept map both contributed to Spencer and her colleagues' development of their conceptual framing of the sets of relationships constitutive of their overarching analytic argument and, as well, provides readers with a visual mapping of the study's key concepts and their dynamic and, as the authors argue, critical interrelationship. This example of a concept map illustrates how it can represent relationships between foundational concepts that, when considered and mapped out together, comprise the core conceptual framework of an empirical study. Using this example helps us to understand that multiple aspects of a researcher's conceptual framework can be mapped out—and worked through—visually and that taken together, these constitute the overarching conceptual framework for the study.

We argue less for a strong emphasis on visual concept mapping per se, believing that researchers have preferred styles of framework development. While we would agree with Maxwell (2005), Miles and Huberman (1994), and others that visually mapping conceptual frameworks can be a quite valuable and clarifying process, we caution students about becoming too focused on the maps at the expense of realizing the value of developing a framework. To the extent that concept maps are generative and focusing, we wholeheartedly support them. When they become an end unto themselves—in other words, when they become viewed as a product rather than a process—we recommend a more narrative approach to concept mapping and conceptual framework development. Ideally, these two approaches go hand in hand. Some of this is determined by how you wrap your mind around the concepts in play (some of us are more visual learners than others) and some of it is shaped by the audiences, both real (dissertation committee) or perceived (the audiences you envision for your published work). However you approach the construction of concept maps, they are an important building block of your conceptual framework and of empirical research more widely.

## RESEARCH MEMOS ☆

Research memos are a long tradition in qualitative research (for discussions and examples of research memos, see Emerson, Fretz, & Shaw, 1995; Marshall & Rossman, 2006; Maxwell, 2005; Miles & Huberman, 1994; Strauss & Corbin, 1990). Research memos have different purposes and formats, but the common goal is to create conscious moments of structured, systematic reflection during the development and implementation of your research project. For example, Maxwell discusses the Researcher Identity Memo as a way to document and examine your intentions, thoughts, goals, and interests as you enter into your research. This type of reflexive memo can be an early-stage approach to research design that helps you identify and engage with aspects of your relationship to your research, but it can also extend well into the research process as it unfolds over time. It can help you focus on your particular, individual influences and contextualize the research endeavor and your researcher identities in relation to broader spheres of influence such as social location and social identity. More broadly, many researchers discuss the use of memos to develop research questions, explore issues of validity, examine the dynamics and undercurrents of research relationships, engage in proposal development, and support and provide structure to the analytic process. For example, Emerson et al. conceive of three primary types of analytic memos: *initial*, *in-process*, and *integrative*. For them, memos are largely focused on the coding of data at the various stages of the analysis process. Memos become a structured place for systematic, structured data analysis at the early, middle, and late stages of coding, theme development, and the emergence of analytical categories and findings. Miles and Huberman cogently describe the role of memos in the analytic process:

> Memos are primarily conceptual in intent. They don't just report data; they tie together different pieces of data into a recognizable cluster, often to show that those data are instances of a general concept. Memos can also go well beyond codes and their relationships to any aspect of the study—personal, methodological, and substantive. They are one of the most useful and powerful sense-making tools at hand. You are writing memos to *yourself*, secondarily to colleagues. . . . Memoing helps the analyst move easily from empirical data to a conceptual level, refining and expanding codes further, developing key categories and showing their relationships, and building toward a more integrated understanding of events, processes, and interaction. (pp. 72–74)

Research memos allow you to choose strategic moments across the research process to delve deeply into specific, substantive issues and layers of analysis in the research. When you examine your research in these kinds of incremental ways throughout the process, the relationships between the various aspects and stages of the research become more visible and valuable. Take for example the following memo written by Michelle Fine concerning her emerging understanding of the guiding concept of hyphenated selves:

Memo: 2/15/07, Musings about Hyphenated Selves
   Why use hyphen as the metaphor—does it reflect a space between like Anzaldua, that connects and separates; that marks fluidity and silos? Does the hyphen serve as an ironic link between two overessentialized identity categories? Might a verb or ellipsis . . . be better, or a hypertext form in which each slice of self is superimaged over/through/with the others, reflecting more creative fusion? But we need a metaphor that has room for the wide range of social psychological furniture these young

people move into the space; the narratives from the young women and men reveal so many wild/contradictory/varied ways to conceptualize how they live the hyphen, what meanings they impute, how they perform in this contentious space between.

In the focus groups, I was just struck by the performance/choreography of diverse social psychological labors at this hyphen—some dance, protest, shiver, hide, invent something new, place scarf on head while others remove, some don a Catholic cross and others grow more religious.

The hyphen offers a theoretical space that can hold politics, ideologies, institutions, relationships, pain, desire, subjectivities, and the intimacies of lives; the metaphor might do us well, as it holds the ambivalence that we need to excavate—a social psychological landscape where those who wander, or are exiled, can choose how they negotiate the land. And then I found material from Roosevelt and Wilson, suggesting the hyphenated identities have long been contested in U.S. debates about citizenship and where lies threat, and for that reason perhaps most significantly it seems important to queer, or reclaim the term. . . . Check this out: Former President Theodore Roosevelt in speaking to the largely Irish Catholic Knights of Columbus at Carnegie Hall on Columbus Day 1915, asserted:

> There is no room in this country for hyphenated Americanism. When I refer to hyphenated Americans, I do not refer to naturalized Americans. Some of the very best Americans I have ever known were naturalized Americans, Americans born abroad. But a hyphenated American is not an American at all. . . . The one absolutely certain way of bringing this nation to ruin, of preventing all possibility of its continuing to be a nation at all, would be to permit it to become a tangle of squabbling nationalities, an intricate knot of German-Americans, Irish-Americans, English-Americans, French-Americans, Scandinavian-Americans or Italian-Americans, each preserving its separate nationality, each at heart feeling more sympathy with Europeans of that nationality, than with the other citizens of the American Republic. . . . There is no such thing as a hyphenated American who is a good American. The only man who is a good American is the man who is an American and nothing else.

President Woodrow Wilson regarded "hyphenated Americans" with suspicion, saying, "Any man who carries a hyphen about with him carries a dagger that he is ready to plunge into the vitals of this Republic whenever he gets ready."

As we can see in this example, memos both result from and contribute to the development of your conceptual framework. They help you maintain focus on your own positionality and the dynamic aspects and issues of research, to delve into the substance of your study as well as your design, to examine your data using different analytic tools and taking different analytic slices of your data to analyze at various stages along the way, and to engage in formative data analysis. Memos, as we can see in Fine's case, are an enormously valuable, generative means of engaging in systematic reflection, analysis, and overall meaning making in your research. They also serve to chronicle and preserve your meaning making as it unfolds, in effect creating a narrative of your analysis process. As we suggested earlier, there are many kinds of and approaches to research memos, from descriptive to analytic, memos that focus on researcher identity, the development of conceptual frameworks, ideological issues, methodological concerns, thematic issues like how issues of power and authority or researcher positionality are instantiated in our research design, implementation, and data analysis (for particularly useful discussions and examples of these kinds of memos see Emerson et al., 1995; Maxwell, 2005). This is not to say that you will need to develop memos on all of these topics. Which memos prove most fruitful will most likely be a function of your research design and the kinds of questions and puzzles you encounter in your data. In each instance, however, the goal is the same: memos are used to both reflect and build on emerging understandings and conceptual frames as researchers engage in the research process.

## ☆ RESEARCH JOURNAL

The research journal is, from our perspective, a generally underutilized but important and valuable research tool. It is a place to examine—in an ongoing and oftentimes unstructured and informal way—thoughts, questions, struggles, ideas, and experiences with the process of learning about and engaging in various aspects of research. A research journal provides a space to engage in ongoing critical questioning as it relates to all facets and stages of the research process. Research journals allow you to (1) develop the good research habit of documenting your work in real time; (2) create opportunities to develop and reflect on questions, concerns, and ideas about the research as they emerge; (3) keep and critically engage with valuable references from the literature in relation to the research topic and methods, which you can incorporate into your emerging theories, the final product, and future research; (4) reflect on your thoughts, interactions, and practices within the researcher role, setting, and process; and (5) formulate and develop ideas for action or changes in approach as they relate to the research process.

For example, in James Spillane's interview about his research, he told us that in the research project that was the focus of Chapter 3 he used what he referred to as "notes to [him]self" (or what we would call a research journal) to chart the development of his understanding of the role of theory in his developing conceptual framework. In describing his more recent work, in which the research is conducted by a team and technology is more evolved than in years passed, Spillane told us that the handwritten notes of years past have been replaced by newer, technology-based strategies.

> In this new study I'm doing, we have a conceptual framework document that's a living document, and it's added to, and we know when it's added to, and we make these decisions and we try and write them down and keep them explicit.

The technology of having a research journal as a public, shared document allows for a more dialogic, generative team approach and makes the insights accessible—and therefore subject to shared inquiry—between and among researchers as the process unfolds.

Similarly, in the interview with Frederick Erickson about his research, he stated that the evolution of his thinking about the conventions and nonneutrality of the transcription process—which significantly influenced the taking up of new directions in his research—emerged through engaging in dialogue with colleagues and in reflective analytic writing over time. From Erickson we can learn an even finer distinction about the role of formalized, written reflection in the generation of data. In his interview, Erickson stated:

> I've been now for some years, as I teach participant observation research . . . , I've been saying that field notes, your stack of field notes aren't data; they're an information source, and you discover data in them by linking pieces of a research question, or an assertion you want to make in, not in question syntax, but in declarative sentence syntax—when you connect an information bit to a research question, then it becomes a datum. While it's just sitting there in the corpus of information materials, it isn't data yet. And so the people who talk about the audiotapes as data—or even field notes as data—I think are actually mistaken.

In this point, we can see the powerful role of a researcher's process of explicating the interpretive process and, even more, the important role of formalizing and chronicling that process of interpretation by writing about it throughout the research process. As Erickson makes clear, analytic meaning making is central to the content and quality of a researcher's data. We argue that this interpretive process must be documented through an organic approach that can capture the complex and often intersecting influences on our thinking as they reside in the nexus of theory, research, and, at times, practice.

As we understand from Spillane's and Erickson's reflections on the role of writing in the interpretive process, research journal entries provide you with an opportunity to engage in less structured but still focused thinking about your research and the literature that forms its context, and, over time, allow you to make deeper connections between the substantive, relational, and contextual issues and realities that emerge throughout the research process. There is not a specific set of rules or guidelines for research journals (unlike memos, which each have a specific set of purposes and goals), but the goal is the real-time, incremental charting of insights and questions as they emerge over time. Some have argued that these entries can be viewed as phenomenological notes that chart your interpretations of the research process, including your own embeddedness in that process (Nakkula & Ravitch, 1998). Others consider them a crucial part of the data collection and analysis process and, in that sense, an essential source of data in empirical studies.

Together, the set of tools we describe here is intended to help you to develop and to get the best possible use out of a conceptual framework. Orienting questions help you to both refine and position your work, while reflective and analytic questions aid in making sense of the research as it unfolds. Concept maps offer a medium for developing and testing ideas about how the main topics or ideas in your research relate to one another. Research memos and journals are tools for diving deeper into specific aspects of your work as it unfolds and for documenting the process itself. Among other things, they help you tell the story of your conceptual framework as it grows and evolves.

## ☆ REASON & RIGOR

As professors and researchers ourselves, we think a great deal about the research process and how to create the conditions necessary for the most rigorous, valid, reliable, respectful, vibrant, authentic, and engaged research possible. We have found in our work that the connective tissue of solid research is the conceptual framework. As guide and ballast, the development of a well-articulated conceptual framework supports your development as a researcher and a scholar. It drives you to articulate your reasons for doing the research you choose to do, and helps you to understand what it means to do that work rigorously. Both are necessary to do exceptional research. Reason without rigor is editorializing; rigor without reason is irrelevant. Ultimately, the utility and impact of your research will be determined by what you have to say, how clearly you can say it, the strength of your argument, and the evidence that supports it. The conceptual framework, we argue, is the clearest, most direct way to produce research that rises to these demands.

# REFERENCES

Abbot, A. (2004). *Methods of discovery: Heuristics for the social sciences.* New York: W. W. Norton.

Anderson, G., & Jones, F. (2000). Knowledge generation in educational administration from the inside out: The promise and perils of site-based, administrator research. *Educational Administration Quarterly, 36,* 428–464.

Anderson, G., & Saavedra, E. (1995). "Insider" narratives of transformative learning: Implications for educational reform. *Anthropology & Education Quarterly, 26,* 228–235.

Anfara, V. A, & Mertz, N. T. (Eds.). (2006). *Theoretical frameworks in qualitative research.* Thousand Oaks, CA: Sage.

Avis, M. (2003). Do we need methodological theory to do qualitative research? *Qualitative Health Research, 13,* 995–1004.

Bailey, D. M., & Jackson, J. M. (2003). Qualitative data analysis: Challenges and dilemmas related to theory and method. *American Journal of Occupational Therapy, 57*(1), 57–65.

Becker, H. (1993). Theory: The necessary evil. In D. J. Flinders & G. E. Mills (Eds.), *Theory and concepts in qualitative research: Perspectives from the field* (pp. 218–229). New York: Teachers College Press.

Biklen, S. K., & Casella, R. (2007). *A practical guide to the qualitative dissertation.* New York: Teachers College Press.

Boote, D. N., & Beile, P. (2005). Scholars before researchers: On the centrality of the literature review in dissertation preparation. *Educational Researcher, 34*(6), 3–15.

Bourdieu, P. (1989). Social space and symbolic power. *Sociological Theory, 7*(1), 14–25.

Bourdieu, P. (1990). *The logic of practice.* Stanford, CA: Stanford University Press. (Original work published 1980)

Bronfenbrenner, U. (1979). *The ecology of human development: Experiments by nature and design.* Cambridge, MA: Harvard University Press.

Brooks, M., & Davies, S. (2007). Pathways to participatory research in developing a tool to measure feelings. *British Journal of Learning Disabilities, 36*(2), 128–133.

Bruce, C. S. (1994). Research students' early experiences of the dissertation literature review. *Studies in Higher Education. 19*(2), 217–229.

Chawla, D. (2006). Subjectivity and the "native" ethnographer: Researcher eligibility in an ethnographic study of urban Indian women in Hindu arranged marriages. *International Journal of Qualitative Methods, 5*(4), 2–13.

Cohen, D. K., & Ball, D. L. (1990). Policy and practice: An overview. *Educational Evaluation and Policy Analysis, 12*, 347–353.

Cohen, D. K., & Barnes, C. A. (1993). Pedagogy and policy. In D. K. Cohen, M. W. McLaughlin, & J. E. Talbert (Eds.), *Teaching for understanding: Challenges for policy and practice* (pp. 207–239). San Francisco: Jossey-Bass.

Cole, M., & Engestrom, Y. (1993). A cultural-historical approach to distributed cognition. In G. Salomon (Ed.), *Distributed cognitions: Psychological and educational considerations* (pp. 1–47). New York: Cambridge University Press.

Creswell, J. (2005). *Research design: Qualitative, quantitative, and mixed methods approaches* (2nd ed.). Thousand Oaks, CA: Sage.

Crotty, M. (1998). *The foundations of social research: Meaning and perspective in the research process.* Thousand Oaks, CA: Sage.

Denzin, N., & Lincoln, Y. (2003). *Collecting and interpreting qualitative materials* (2nd ed.). Thousand Oaks, CA: Sage.

Dressman, M. (2008). *Using social theory in educational research: A practical guide.* London: Routledge.

Elmore, R. F., & McLaughlin, M. W. (1988). *Steady work: Policy, practice and the reform of American education.* Santa Monica, CA: Rand.

Erickson, F. (1996). Going for the zone: The social and cognitive ecology of teacher-student interaction in classroom conversations. In D. Hicks (Ed.), *Discourse, learning, and schooling* (pp. 29–62). Cambridge, UK: Cambridge University Press.

Erickson, F. (2004). *Talk and social theory: Ecologies of speaking and listening in everyday life.* Cambridge, UK: Polity Press.

Emerson, R. M., Fretz, R. I., & Shaw, L. L. (1995). *Writing ethnographic fieldnotes.* Chicago: University of Chicago Press.

Fine, M., & Sirin, S. R. (2007). Theorizing hyphenated selves: Researching youth development in and across contentious political contexts. *Social and Personality Psychology Compass, 1*, 1–23.

Fine, M., Torre, M.E., Boudin, K., Bowen, I., Clark, J., Hytton, D., et al. (2001). *Changing minds: The impact of college in a maximum-security prison. Effects on women in prison, the prison environment, reincarceration rates and post-release outcomes.* New York: City University of New York.

Flinders, D., & Mills, G. (Eds.). (1993). *Theory and concepts in qualitative research: Perspectives from the field.* New York: Teachers College Press.

Fordham, S. (1996). *Blacked out: Dilemmas of race, identity, and success at Capital High.* Chicago: University of Chicago Press.

Gadamer, H.-G. (1989). *Truth and method* (2nd ed.). New York: Crossroad.

Glesne, C. (2006). *Becoming qualitative researchers: An introduction.* Boston: Pearson/Allyn & Bacon.

Goar, C. (2008). Experiments in black and white: Power and privilege in experimental methodology. In T. Zuberi & E. Bonilla-Silva (Eds.), *White logic, white methods: Racism and methodology* (pp. 153–162). Lanham, MD: Rowman & Littlefield.

Golafshani, N. (2003). Understanding reliability and validity in qualitative research. *The Qualitative Report, 8*, 597–607. Retrieved from http://www.nova.edu/ssss/QR/QR8-4/golafshani.pdf

Greeno, J., Collins, A., & Resnick, L. (1996). Cognition and learning. In D. Berliner & R. Calfee (Eds.), *Handbook of educational psychology* (pp. 15–46). New York: Simon & Schuster.

Greenwood, D. J., & Levin, M. (1998). *Introduction to action research.* Thousand Oaks, CA: Sage.

Guba, E. (1990). *The paradigm dialogue.* Newbury Park, CA: Sage.

Hammersley, M., & Atkinson, P. (2007). *Ethnography.* New York: Routledge.

Harrison, J., MacGibbon, L., & Morton, M. (2001). Regimes of trustworthiness in qualitative research: The rigors of reciprocity. *Qualitative Inquiry, 7*, 323–346.

Hart, C. (1998). *Doing a literature review: Releasing the social science research imagination.* London: Sage.

Jaffee, S., Kling, K. C., Plant, E. A., Sloan, M., & Hyde, J. S. (1999). The view from down here: Feminist graduate students consider innovative methodologies. *Psychology of Women Quarterly, 23*, 423–430.

Jencks, C. F. (1995). *The homeless.* Cambridge, MA: Harvard University Press.

Langdridge, D. (2007). *Phenomenological psychology: Theory, research and method.* Harlow, UK: Pearson Education.

Lave, J., & Wenger, E. (1991). *Situated learning: Legitimate peripheral participation.* Cambridge, UK: Cambridge University Press.

Leshem, S. (2007). Thinking about conceptual frameworks in a research community of practice: A case of a doctoral programme. *Innovations in Education and Teaching International, 44*, 287–299.

Liiv, K. E. (1998). Another backward arc: Further reflections on "expert" and "problem." In M. J. Nakkula & S. M. Ravitch (Eds.), *Matters of interpretation: Reciprocal transformation in therapeutic and developmental relationships with youth* (pp. 137–151). San Francisco: Jossey-Bass.

Locke, L. F., Spirduso, W. W., & Silverman, S. J. (2007). *Proposals that work: A guide to planning dissertations and grant proposals.* Thousand Oaks, CA: Sage.

Lytle, S. L., & Cochran-Smith, M. (1992). Teacher research as a way of knowing. *Harvard Educational Review, 62*, 447–474.

Marshall, C., & Rossman, G. B. (2006). *Designing qualitative research* (4th ed.). Thousand Oaks, CA: Sage.

Maxwell, J. A. (2005). *Qualitative research design: An interactive approach* (2nd ed.). Thousand Oaks, CA: Sage.

Maxwell, J. A. (2006). Literature reviews of, and for, educational research: A commentary on Boote and Beile's "Scholars before researchers." *Educational Researcher, 35*(9), 28–31.

Maxwell, J. A. (2010). Review of *Theory and Educational Research* by Jean Anyon. *Education Review, 13*. Retrieved from http://www.edrev.info/reviews/rev882.pdf

Maxwell, J. A., & Mittapalli, K. (2010). Realism as a stance for mixed methods research. In A. Tashakkori & C. Teddlie (Eds.), *Handbook of mixed methods in social and educational research* (pp. 145–167). Thousand Oaks, CA: Sage.

Maxwell, J. A. (in press.). *A realist approach for qualitative research*. Thousand Oaks, CA: Sage.

Maxwell, J. A., & Mittapalli, K. (2008). Theory. In L. Given (Ed.), *The SAGE encyclopedia of qualitative research methods* (pp. 876–880). Thousand Oaks, CA: SAGE Publications.

Miles, M. B., & Huberman, M. A. (1994). *Qualitative data analysis: An expanded sourcebook* (2nd ed.). Thousand Oaks, CA: Sage.

Mills, S. (2003). *Michel Foucault*. New York: Routledge.

Morse, J. M. (2004). Constructing qualitatively derived theory: Concept construction and concept typologies. *Qualitative Health Research, 13,* 1387–1395.

Nakkula, M. J., & Ravitch, S. M. (1998). *Matters of interpretation: Reciprocal transformation in therapeutic and developmental relationships with youth*. San Francisco: Jossey-Bass.

Noffke, S. (1999). What's a nice theory like yours doing in a practice like this? And other impertinent questions about practitioner research. *Change: Transformations in Education, 2*(1), 25–35.

Norris, N. (1997). Error, bias, and validity in qualitative research. *Education Action Research, 5*(1), 172–176.

Nunan, D. (1992). *Research methods in language learning*. New York: Cambridge University Press.

Parker, L., & Lynn, M. (2002). What's race got to do with it? Critical Race Theory's conflicts with and connections to qualitative research methodology and epistemology. *Qualitative Inquiry, 8*(1), 7–22.

Peshkin, A. (1988). In search of subjectivity—one's own. *Educational Researcher, 17*(7), 17–22.

Ravitch, S. M. (2000). *"Reading myself between the lines": White teachers reading, writing and talking about issues of diversity, inequality and pedagogy*. Unpublished doctoral dissertation, University of Pennsylvania.

Ravitch, S. M., & Wirth, K. (2007). Collaborative development of a pedagogy of opportunity for urban students: Navigations and negotiations in insider action research. *Journal of Action Research, 5*(1), 75–91.

Richardson, V. (1999). Teacher education and the construction of meaning. In G. Griffin (Ed.), *The education of teachers* (pp. 145–166). Chicago: University of Chicago Press.

Ricoeur, P. (1973). The task of hermeneutics. *Philosophy Today, 17*(2/4), 112–128.

Russell, G. M., & Bohan, J. S. (1999). Hearing voices: The uses of research and the politics of change. *Psychology of Women Quarterly, 23,* 403–418.

Schön, D. (1995). The new scholarship requires a new epistemology. *Change, 27,* 26–34.

Schram, T. H. (2003). *Conceptualizing qualitative inquiry*. Columbus, OH: Merrill Prentice Hall.

Schwandt, T. (1993). Theory for the moral sciences: Crisis of identity and purpose. In D. J. Flinders & G. E. Mills (Eds.), *Theory and concepts in qualitative research: Perspectives from the field* (pp. 5–23). New York: Teachers College Press.

Schwandt, T. A. (2007). *Dictionary of qualitative inquiry* (3rd ed.). Thousand Oaks, CA: Sage.

Shulman, L. S. (1999). Professing educational scholarship. In E. C. Lagemann & L. S. Shulman (Eds.), *Issues in education research: Problems and possibilities* (pp. 159–165). San Francisco: Jossey-Bass.

Sirin, S. R., & Fine, M. (2007). Hyphenated selves: Muslim American youth negotiating identities on the fault lines of global conflict *Applied Development Science, 11*(3), 151–163.

Skeggs, B. (2001). Feminist ethnography. In P. Atkinson, A. Coffey, S. Delamont, J. Lofland, & L. Lofland (Eds.), *Handbook of ethnography* (pp. 426–442). Thousand Oaks, CA: Sage.

Spencer, M. B. (2008). Phenomenology and ecological systems theory: Development of diverse groups. In W. Damon & R. Lerner (Eds.), *Child and adolescent development: An advanced course* (pp. 696–740). New York: John Wiley & Sons.

Spencer, M., Dupree, D., & Hartmann, T. (1997). A Phenomenological Variant of Ecological Systems Theory (PVEST): A self-organizational perspective in context. *Development and Psychopathology, 9*, 817–833.

Spencer, M. B., Harpalani, V., Cassidy, E., Jacobs, C. Y., Donde, S., Goss, T. N., et al. (2006). Understanding vulnerability and resilience from a normative developmental perspective: Implications for racially and ethnically diverse youth. In D. Cicchetti & D. J. Cohen (Eds.), *Developmental psychopathology* (pp. 627–672). Hoboken, NJ: John Wiley & Sons.

Spillane, J. (1996). Districts matter: Local educational authorities and state instructional policy. *Educational Policy, 10*(1), 63–87.

Spillane, J. (1998). The progress of standards-based reforms and the non-monolithic nature of the local school district: Organizational and professional considerations. *American Educational Research Journal, 35*(1), 33–63.

Spillane, J. (1999). External reform initiatives and teachers' efforts to reconstruct their practice: The mediating role of teachers' zones of enactment. *Journal of Curriculum Studies, 31*(2), 143–175.

Spillane, J. (2000). Cognition and policy implementation: District policy-makers and the reform of mathematics education. *Cognition and Instruction, 18*(2), 141–179.

Spillane, J. (2002). Local theories of teacher change: The pedagogy of district policies and programs. *Teachers College Record, 104*, 377–420.

Spillane, J. (2004). *Standards deviation: How schools misunderstand education policy.* Cambridge, MA: Harvard University Press.

Spillane, J. (2006). *Distributed leadership.* San Francisco: Jossey-Bass.

Spillane, J., & Diamond, J. (Eds.). (2007). *Distributed leadership in practice.* New York: Teachers College Press.

Spillane, J. P., & Zeuli, J. S. (1999). Reform and mathematics teaching: Exploring patterns of practice in the context of national and state reforms. *Educational Evaluation and Policy Analysis,* 21(1), 1–27.

Strauss, A. (1995). Notes on the nature and development of general theories. *Qualitative Inquiry, 1*(1), 7–18.

Strauss, A., & Corbin, J. (1990). *Basics of qualitative research: Grounded theory procedures and techniques.* London: Sage.

Van Maanen, J. (1988). *Tales of the field: On writing ethnography.* Chicago: University of Chicago Press.

# AUTHOR INDEX

# SUBJECT INDEX

# SAGE Research Methods Online

## The essential tool for researchers

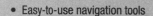